ASK ADAM

BY Barbara Joyce Bush

I Can't Stand Cindy, Lord!
Ask Adam

ASK ADAM

A Shepherd and His Flock
Face the Wolves Together

Barbara Joyce Bush

FLEMING H. REVELL COMPANY
Old Tappan, New Jersey

Library of Congress Cataloging in Publication Data

Bush, Barbara.
   Ask Adam.

   I. Title.
PZ4.B9777As [PS3552.U816]   813'.5'4   78-8267
ISBN 0-8007-0942-X

TO my parents, with eternal gratitude that among all the good and loving deeds of their lives, they did not neglect the greatest: seeing to it that their children were introduced to Jesus Christ.

Contents

1

Patch Up My Affairs

Adam watched as the car, with headlights shining in the twilight, cautiously edged its way toward the driveway and into the church parking lot. It was just as he thought. He had not recognized the name of the man who had telephoned so urgently for a very good reason—the man was a stranger. He sighed and tried to add a line to his article for the newsletter, but the tension of waiting for the secretary's brief knock and the anticipation of the interview broke his concentration. Unfamiliar with the building, the gentleman took even longer than usual to find the office, but, eventually, the tap sounded.

"Come in," he called.

Sally Jacobs opened the door wide. "Mr. Carson is here," she announced pleasantly, and a stockily built man of about forty entered the room. He stood about five nine, for when Adam came from behind his desk to shake hands, he had to look down slightly into Carson's eyes. Adam's suspicions had been correct in another area as well. The man had been drinking, and that always complicated the counseling situation.

Sally lingered at the door, eyebrows elevated inquiringly. Adam smiled at her.

"Thank you, Sally," he said, and nodded encouragingly. She might as well go home. The man didn't look

11

belligerent, and she had a family who would undoubtedly need dinner before much longer.

As the door closed, Adam settled himself into the up-
holstered chair which was a twin to the one Mr. Carson
had chosen. When it appeared that the visitor was too
nervous to begin, Adam took the initiative.

"What can I do for you, Mr. Carson?"

"Call me Ralph, please, Reverend Dunn."

"Okay, Ralph, and you call me Adam. Now, how can I
help you?"

Ralph Carson fidgeted as if trying to find a comfortable
position. He reached down and pulled up each sock a
notch, and Adam could see that his sandy hair was thin
on top. Finally he began.

"You see, I have this problem . . . ." He shifted
again, eyes now fixed on a section of carpet. "I have this
problem," he repeated, "and I don't know anyone who
can help me. I drive by this church here every day. And I
got to thinking, maybe a reverend could do the trick, you
know?" He glanced up for the first time, pulling at his
shirt collar, which was too tight, even without the tie.

"What is your problem?" Adam prompted.

"Well, me and my wife have been divorced over five
years now, and, well, it gets lonely, you know?" Ralph
looked up again, reading what he could of Adam's reaction to this much of his story.

Adam thought he could see where the conversation
was heading—drinking to deaden the pain of isolation
and loss. "Loneliness is not easy to deal with," he responded.

"It sure isn't. Anyway, about two years ago I met this
gal over at The Willows, and we hit if off pretty good."

"Do you work at The Willows?"

"No, no. Neither of us do. I guess we both just happened in at the same time, you know, to have a drink and

a couple of laughs before we had to go put a TV dinner in the oven again . . . ."

And you want me to marry you, Adam thought but waited for Ralph to continue.

"Anyway, me and this gal—her name is Della—me and Della hit it off pretty good, and one thing led to another, and we finally decided to, you know, have a go at it and see if something worked out for us. I mean, a person's got to get something out of life, doesn't he? When your wife ups and leaves you, you don't just stop living, you know?" The combination of alcohol and self-pity gave his voice a whine.

"So you and this woman began living together?"

Ralph nodded.

"Has Della been married before also?" he asked for no particular reason. It just seemed he ought to ask something.

Ralph hesitated. "I . . . don't . . . think so," he answered, and his demeanor showed that to him the point was not relevant to his problem.

Adam wondered if he should call Trudi and check in about dinner but decided it wasn't that late yet.

"Well, anyway, it wasn't any time at all until Della started acting just like my wife used to!" He paused to let this remarkable fact sink in. "She began griping, griping that I never had enough money. She took my credit cards and ran up bills all over town, and she was still on me to get more money, more money!" Ralph was agitated now, gesturing animatedly as his recital continued. "I even got a second job, but that didn't shut her up, either. She was still after me all the time about how I didn't make enough dough, complaining about how much I sent to my ex-wife and kids. I tried to make her understand that I *had* to send that money or I'd have the courts on my neck, but she wouldn't listen to me." He sat back lost in thought, shaking his head in disbelief at such injustice.

After a few moments, he leaned forward suddenly and looked Adam in the face. The liquor smell was even more pronounced at closer range. "And *then* what do you think she did?" he demanded. "She up and left me! Just packed her things—some of them not even paid for yet—and walked out on me. Can you believe that?"

Adam could, easily. But before he could reply, Ralph continued.

"Man, was I burned. I mean, I gave her everything I could, and she still walks out on me. I was really steamed." Suddenly Ralph slumped back into the chair, all the fight gone. He sat dejectedly for a minute before adding in a colorless voice, "That was last week. She left me Friday."

Where do I start with this one, Lord? Adam prayed. *You must have brought him here for some reason. I'd better say something, before he gets maudlin and starts crying.*

But Ralph sat up and, to Adam's surprise, looked at his watch. "We've got to get going here," he said briskly. "You see, reverend, I really need this woman. I want her to come back to me. So I left work early and went over to The Willows, and, sure enough, she was there. I tried to talk her into coming back to me, but she wouldn't hear of it. Said she was sick of scrounging around and if I really wanted her, I'd give her back my credit cards. I told her I'd look for a better-paying job, but I can't get it through to her that salesmen's jobs aren't hanging from every tree. She just won't listen to reason!" Ralph edged forward in his chair. "That's when I thought about you."

"Me?"

"Right. I thought, if she won't listen to me, maybe she'll listen to a reverend. So I went to the telephone booth and looked up Cavalry Church."

"Calvary," Adam corrected.

"Beg your pardon?"

"It's *Calvary* Church, not Cavalry. Calvary is the name of the place where Jesus was crucified."

"Oh, right. Seen your sign lots of times. That's how I knew who to call. Anyway, reverend, I figure you're the only one who can help me. She'd listen to you."

"Why should she listen to me? She's never met me."

"But you're a preacher! You're supposed to listen to preachers!"

Adam looked at his visitor speculatively. "Would *you* listen to me, Ralph?"

"Well . . . sure . . . . Of course I would!"

"Then I'm going to tell you something, Ralph, since you are sure you'll listen. I'm going to tell you that you are looking to the wrong person, trying to find an answer to your loneliness. No human being will ever make you happy. But God cares about you. He wants to *give* to you, not *use* you. Jesus Christ can be your personal friend."

Ralph Carson glanced nervously at his watch. "I told her I'd be right back. If we don't hurry, she might be gone."

"Let me make sure I understand this, Ralph. You want me to come back to the bar with you and try to persuade a woman to whom you are not married into coming back and living with you."

Ralph nodded vigorously. "Tell her I'm really okay. Tell her I really will try to get a better job. Tell her how much I need her." He was anxious to get going, now that they understood each other.

"I'm afraid I can't do what you want me to, Ralph."

"What? Why not?"

"Well, first of all, I don't know you. I can't go promise someone you will do certain things, because I don't know if you will." Ralph started to object, but Adam raised his hand in a silencing gesture and continued. "But more importantly, the Bible says that your relationship with this woman is an adulterous one. God forbids adultery. It is sin. As a minister of Jesus Christ, I cannot promote a relationship which He condemns."

"I tried to get her to marry me, but she wouldn't!"

"That is not the problem, Ralph. Your whole situation is unhealthy. You have left out God at every point; so there is no hope for fulfillment."

Ralph looked at his watch again, then said resentfully, "If you won't help me, I've got no place else to turn. I thought the church was supposed to help people in need."

"I am trying to help you. But doing what you are asking will not help you . . . ."

"Yes it will. It really will."

"No, Ralph. Only God knows what will make you happy. He made you, and He knows what you really need. You need Him in your life. Otherwise you will just go from one bad experience to another."

"Della and me could make a go of it. I know we could."

"God says no."

"How do *you* know what God says?" Ralph shot back angrily. "You think you're the only one in this world with a pipeline to heaven?" He got to his feet indignantly. "I've just been wasting my time. Some help you are!" He began backing toward the door. "I guess I came to the wrong place. If that's all you've got to say, then thanks but no thanks, preacher!" he shouted and slammed the door.

Adam had risen also, but now sank back into the chair. *Lord, it's impossible to get through to them. They are so blind.* He felt drained and weary. Before long he saw

Ralph's car screech out the driveway and turn right without so much as a token pause. There was no hesitancy in his direction. He knew where he was going, back to The Willows and to Della.

Adam got up, arranged a few things on his desk, then went to the door. He would be late for dinner if he didn't get moving, and the class for new members started at seven-thirty.

2

Organize Programs in Case I Want to Use Them

Trudi was relieved to hear the car pull into the garage. She had started the chops at six-thirty, certain that Adam would have called if he were going to cut it any closer. The boys' TV programs were over, and for the last half hour, they had been into the kitchen every five minutes, asking when dinner would be ready.

The door from the garage opened and closed. She heard Adam's keys clinking as he slid them into his pocket. Several moments followed when she heard only the stove's exhaust fan, and she knew he was shuffling through the day's mail which routinely lay on the stereo. Trudi was stirred inwardly as she followed her husband's movements by sound. *If anything ever happened to him,* she thought, *this would be one of the hardest parts to adjust to—waiting for familiar sounds that never came.*

Adam entered the kitchen, letters still in hand, and Trudi turned to greet him with a kiss.

"How's it going, honey?" she asked.

"Oh, fine."

"Been out calling?"

"No, a guy came by the office late."

"Anybody I know?"

"Nope. Nobody I know either."

"What?"

"A guy called from a bar and said he had to see me right away. Of course, I didn't know where he was calling from until later. Anyway, I said okay, and I'll bet you can't guess what he wanted?"

Trudi considered for a moment. "Money for another drink?"

"Wrong. He wanted me to come back to the bar with him and talk this woman who had been living with him into coming back and living with him some more."

"You're kidding!"

"Nope."

"Was he drunk?" Trudi set the filled serving dishes on the table.

"No, just 'under the influence.' "

"I suppose you were all alone with him." Trudi said with an edge to her voice.

Matt and Tim ran into the kitchen, each claiming one of their father's arms. He broke loose and ruffled the hair on each head. "Hi, kids, how're you doing?" he greeted them, and then returned to the original conversation. "It was all right. He wasn't the mean kind."

"Not even when he left?"

Adam began washing his hands at the kitchen sink. "As a matter of fact," he admitted, "he was a little upset there at the end." Adam dried his hands and sat down at the table as the boys scurried to their places.

"The really discouraging thing is, most people don't have any more idea of what the church is all about than this guy did. They seem to think a minister is some kind of community counseling service. You'd think my salary came out of tax funds."

"That's why I wish you had someone around

whenever you're dealing with unstable people. Look what they did to Jesus when He turned out to be something different from what they wanted Him to be."

Adam smiled wryly. "I don't think it will come to that."

"No, but don't try to tell me they won't act irrationally if you won't go along with them, because I've been there and seen the look in their eyes."

Adam patted her hand. "Don't get so upset, honey. I usually do have somebody around, and we both know the Lord is in charge."

Trudi nodded resignedly—*who could argue with that?*—and sat down as they bowed their heads to give thanks for their meal.

After Tim and Matt had reported on their second- and third-grade activities, Trudi asked if Adam had seen the note about the Turners.

"Yes. They won't be at membership class. Did they say why?"

"No, she just said they wouldn't be there tonight."

"When did she call?"

"About three this afternoon."

"I was at the office then. I wonder why she didn't call there. They weren't at the class last week either. That's two absences out of six right off the bat. I guess I'm going to have to suggest they drop out and catch the next series."

"Always some like that, isn't there?"

"Yep." Adam finished his last bite and got up. "Sorry to rush in and out, but I'll barely get the place opened up as it is." Trudi stood, raised her face for a parting kiss and gave him an extra hug before he left.

Tom Aiken was waiting on the walk to the side entrance when Adam drove up. It lifted Adam's spirit just

to see him. The elders shared in leading the sessions for
new members, fulfilling one of their many teaching func-
tions. Tom had served on the Pastor-Seeking Committee
that had recommended Adam to the congregation and
had become one of the people he turned to most often for
wisdom and prayer support. Another minister had once
told him, "You'll be lucky if half the committee is still
speaking to you after the first year." Adam was grateful
that things had turned out so much better than that,
though he was close to few as he was to Tom.

"How come you're here on time? Thought the meeting started at seven?" he called as he got out of the car,
knowing full well Tom had probably driven straight to
church from work and had not even stopped to eat.

"You can't blame a guy for trying to make a good impression, can you?" Tom retorted.

Adam made his way up the cement strip. "You're
really worried about your job security around here,
aren't you?" They shook hands. "Good to see you,
buddy," Adam said, then unlocked the heavy double
doors and propped one open. "I forgot to start the coffee
before I left for home, so I'll have to get it going now.
Greet any that come, will you, and see that they get their
name badges off the table there."

The Pastor's Classes for prospective members met in
one of the rooms near the church offices. Sally had pre-
pared the large coffee maker; so Adam only had to carry
it from the sink area in the workroom into the meeting
room and plug it in.

The newer units of the church plant had been built in
the late sixties. The older facilities had been erected
about ten years before that. They contained several
classrooms plus the former sanctuary, which was used
now as a fellowship hall. The more recent addition had
doubled the classroom space and added a large office

section and permanent sanctuary.

Adam had been impressed that the congregation in its formative years had been farsighted enough to purchase land to accommodate much future growth. This zeal and planning throughout the church's life was one of the things used by God to draw him to this people.

Adam believed churches were supposed to grow. He believed churches true to the Word of God did grow. He was excited to find that this group of Christians also wanted to keep expanding and reaching new people for Christ. He had been their pastor for three years now, and he was sure their faithfulness and sanctified optimism continued to feed his spirit at least as much as his determination to declare the whole counsel of God fed theirs.

The problems that had arisen had tended to draw the leaders together in study and prayer rather than divide them. So far, there had been no major, agonizing disruptions. But Adam knew that anywhere spiritual progress was being made, Satan stepped up his artillery. This was one of the few anxieties about the church that repeatedly assailed him, and he found himself often praying for the grace and courage to sustain them all through whatever crises lay ahead.

Trudi had said on several occasions, "I don't know how you can keep going over and over that material with each new members' class." But to Adam the groups were one of the more satisfying parts of his ministry. Growth was his vision, and they signified growth.

The participants generally represented a wide range of Christian experience: young couples realizing their need of a more disciplined relationship with Christ for the first time since they had left their parents' homes; older couples who had walked with the Lord for years; teenagers who had come to faith in Jesus through the Sunday school or at summer camp; widows and widow-

ers seeking a fellowship of believers; several who had
not yet been claimed by Christ but who wanted to find
out what motivated this unusual bunch of people. It was
never taken for granted that all who attended the classes
would end up joining. On the contrary, almost every
batch of participants included those who, for various
reasons, decided not to take the final step toward membership.

Why people would sign up to come, as the Turners
had, and then not show up remained a mystery to Adam.
He had known of some instances where one half of the
couple had taken the initiative by enrolling both of them,
hoping that when the time came, the spouse would agree
to attend, also. This seldom worked. He did not think
that was the case with the Turners and decided a visit to
them would be in order.

When he returned with the coffeepot, Tom Aiken's
wife, Eileen, had arrived and was introducing herself to
some of those beginning to gather. The elders' wives had
not originally been included in the membership classes,
but several had complained that they were getting to
know too few of the new people; so Adam had been
delighted to have them come on the night their husbands
took part.

The evening went well. Tom and Adam split the class
into two groups for a discussion on the nature of the
church, using three metaphors for the church found in
the New Testament: Body of Christ, bride of Christ,
household of God.

After everyone else had gone home, Tom lingered. As
he helped Adam gather and put away the materials he
said, "Has Liz Armstrong been in to see you?"

"How recently?"

"Within the last day or two."

Adam shook his head. "No . . . some problem?"

"She's worried about the Kleinschmidts. It seems Mrs. Kleinschmidt didn't show up at a luncheon or a morning Bible study, and the girls haven't been to the high-school group this week either."

"No reason given?"

"Liz called twice and said Christine sounded terrible but wouldn't talk, which makes her think it's really serious. Are both husband and wife members?"

"No, only Christine. Claus came to all the classes, but she and the girls joined without him."

"That's what I thought. They've been pretty faithful, haven't they?"

"She and the daughters have been. Claus attends about once a month. He always sits with his arms folded across his chest, apparently taking in every word I say. But he never seems moved, one way or the other."

"I've never gotten more than a hello out of him."

Adam picked up the coffee maker and headed down the hall to the sink. Tom carried the tray with cream, sugar, spoons, and napkins.

"I guess I'd better drop by in the next day or two." Adam sighed. "But I expect it's just hurt feelings over something or other. Did I tell you about the father that came storming in here last night?"

"No. What was the trouble?"

"It was about ten minutes after nine, and a man I'd never seen before came in through the door there and said, 'Why can't you people get things together around here!' "

"What was that all about?"

"It turned out he was a fellow who had no connections with the church at all except his kid comes to the junior-high youth group. So here he was. His son had been treated to recreation, refreshments, music, and Bible lesson, all by dedicated volunteers, and he was fit

to be tied, because the teacher ran over five or ten minutes, and he was missing his TV program. I mean, he was
yelling at me!"

"What did you say?"

"I don't even remember. Not what I felt like saying, of
course. I'm sure he thinks I'm the typical patsy minister
you see in the movies—all folded hands and sickly
smiles."

Tom laughed. "I don't imagine you looked *that*
docile."

Adam grinned back at him. "No, I don't suppose I did.
The 'old man' was banging so hard to get out that the guy
probably got a glimpse of him at that."

The two of them returned through the building, turning off lights and checking doors as they went. "Anyway,
it's probably more of the same with Kleinschmidts,"
Adam added, "but I'll drop by and see what's going on."

They walked toward the parking lot. Adam said, "Tell
Eileen how much I appreciate her coming."

"I will. She knows it."

"And get some dinner."

"I will." He smiled. "I needed to diet anyway."

"Sure, sure." Adam put a hand on his friend's shoul-
der. "It's good to be with you, Tom."

"The feeling is mutual. See you Sunday." He walked
to his car.

"God bless you tomorrow at work," Adam called, got
into his own car, and followed Tom out of the parking lot
to the street, where they parted ways.

3

Overcome Evil With Good

Adam was wrong about the Kleinschmidts. He knew it the moment Christine opened the door, and he saw the bedraggled housecoat, the swollen eyelids, and blank, expressionless face.

"Hello, Pastor Dunn," she said and stood as if in a trance.

"May I come in, Christine?" he asked gently.

She hesitated, then nodded and unhooked the screen. Adam let himself in, followed her into the living room and sat in a chair opposite the couch she had chosen.

"Are Doris and Ginnie still at school?"

She shook her head. "They're at my folks'. I had to get them away . . . ." She sat, teary eyed, gazing unseeingly out a window.

"Why don't you tell me what's wrong, Christine? Several people are concerned about you and would like to help you."

"No one can help!" She blurted out in a voice cracking with emotion, then subsiding into a whisper. "It's all so horrible. So horrible. I can't believe it."

"I've heard many horrible things before, Christine. You really should not try to carry whatever it is alone."

She twisted a tissue around and around her finger. "If only I'd paid attention. I knew something was wrong lately. Ginnie and I have always been so close. I *knew* something was wrong, but I just didn't pay enough attention!"

"It's something to do with Ginnie?"

Christine began weeping again, and Adam thought he had never seen anyone so broken. He waited, afraid to press in the state she was in. Finally she roused herself.

"You know Claus is not the girls' father."

Adam was surprised at this turn in the conversation. "Yes, I guess I remember that now."

"So you see, it's all my fault, *all* my fault. I just never dreamed . . . ."

"Where is Claus now? Shouldn't he be here with you?"

Christine raised her head, her eyes full of fire and hate. "He's in jail where he belongs!" she rasped.

Adam was dumbfounded. "In jail! What for?"

"Can't you see? Don't you *understand?*" she wailed. Words spurted out between racking sobs. "Ginnie wasn't sure . . . afraid to tell . . . she couldn't believe . . . until Thursday night . . . ."

Adam moved over to the couch and held onto the jerking form beside him. After she had quieted a bit, still not believing he grasped the situation, he ventured, "You're trying to tell me that Claus has been making advances toward Ginnie?"

Christine nodded. "If only I'd paid more attention . . . if I had just realized . . . ." Adam felt physically ill. The woman was right. It was too horrible to believe, especially about someone you knew and particularly involving someone as impressionable as fifteen-year-old Ginnie. He had thought he had been through every pos-

sible situation during his years in the ministry—
abortion, homosexuality, murder. It had not been the
sheltered life he had assumed it would be. But this was
one circumstance he had never had to deal with before.
He continued to hold onto her arms, afraid she would
literally come apart with grief.

"You shouldn't be alone, Christine. Has anyone been
here with you?"

She shook her head.

"Liz Armstrong has been concerned about you. Why
don't I call her and see if she can come sit with you for a
while?"

"No! I don't wany *anyone* to know, not *anyone!*"

"I'm sure you don't, Christine. I understand that, but
you need someone, anyway. You could trust Liz completely. Or how about Trudi? Trudi would want to be
with you, I know. You could be sure she would never say
a word to anyone." He paused but saw no response.
"Why don't I call Trudi and ask her to come over for a
while? Would that be all right with you?"

She nodded listlessly. Adam went to the telephone
before she could change her mind, praying Trudi would
be at home. Thankfully, she was. He spoke as softly as
possible.

"Honey? This is really important. Get someone to
watch the boys right away and come to the
Kleinschmidts'. Do you know where they live? Good."
He filled her in briefly, hung up, and returned to find
Christine much calmer.

"I want you to know that I think Ginnie got away . . .
before the worst. She says she did . . . . It was my
bowling night . . . ." She was struggling for control but
seemed to need to continue talking now that the crime
was out in the open.

"She ran across the street to her girlfriend's house.

They don't know what happened. At least Ginnie said she didn't tell them. But she was crying and shaking, they said; so they had her stay there till I got home. I don't know what they think. Doris was studying at a friend's. When I got home, no one was here. That seemed funny, but I didn't think much about it . . . until the neighbors brought Ginnie home." Her emotions overcame her again, and it was some time before she could continue.

"After I finally got her to tell me, I called the police. I didn't want him to come back here! They arrested him when he pulled up outside."

"You could have called me then, Christine. No one should try to go through something like this alone."

"I just couldn't." She had relapsed into a panicky whisper, and Adam strove to prevent a return to her former despair by speaking calmly but firmly.

"I think I understand how you feel about it. It is an evil thing, and you are ashamed. You feel guilty, because you think you should have prevented it. But, Christine, Christians from the first century until now have had to combat all kinds of wickedness, both in their own lives and forced upon them from the world around them. No real Christian would feel anything but compassion and a sharing of your grief." It appeared that she was hearing him, but he was not sure. He pushed on hopefully. "Satan attacks us every way he can, and we absolutely must draw together and not let him have any more victory in this than he already has. Are you going to let him drive you away from God's people through this? That's what he wants, you know."

Christine raised her head, and for the first time since he had arrived, looked at him squarely. Her face was blotchy and puffy, and her eyes almost entirely red. "I never thought of it that way," she replied more composedly, and he felt her brain was at last beginning to function.

"And Ginnie will need continuing assurances from you that she is not at fault somehow. As her mother, you must help her deal with this and then put it behind her and not let it keep on frightening her."

This statement had its desired effect, for Adam could see her starting to focus on Ginnie's needs rather than on her own overwhelming sense of guilt.

The doorbell sounded. "I'll get it," Adam said, rising. "It's probably Trudi."

Trudi was standing on the porch, and she looked at Adam enquiringly as he held the door open for her. "Christine's feeling a little better now," he said loudly enough for the woman to hear easily.

Trudi went over to the distressed woman, sat down beside her, and put her arms around her. "Oh, Chris, I'm so sorry," she said and just held her for several moments. "You know we'll do everything we can to help, don't you?" Christine nodded and reached for another tissue.

Adam sat with them for several more minutes before making his exit. As he was leaving, Trudi slipped over to him. "The boys are next door, and there is chicken and rice in the crockery pot on the counter in case I'm here late."

He nodded and left. He was always grateful for women he could call in at crucial moments, but he relied especially on Trudi. Christine would unload on Trudi far more than she could bring herself to reveal to him yet, and it was vital to get as much of the foulness as possible up from the deep crevices of her mind and out into the healing light.

Adam headed for the Turners'. He was in no hurry for a change, since he had fifteen minutes before he was expected there. He prayed for wisdom for the coming interview, for Trudi as she talked with Christine Kleinschmidt, and for relief from the throbbing ache that was creeping up the back of his neck. As he waited at a red traffic light, he rolled his head around several times in a circle, which helped a little.

Calvin's car was parked in the driveway when Adam pulled up at the curb. He left in the car the materials covering the two membership classes the Turners had missed. If he was convinced they would attend the remaining four segments, he would come back and get them.

Adam perceived an element of strain in the greeting he received. This could signify several things: *they* might be upset, or they might be worried that *he* was upset. He guessed their ages to be in the early forties. Both were above average in height and had thin, somewhat angular frames.

Trying to warm the atmosphere, Adam admired a particularly striking stitchery design which graced the living-room wall. Elizabeth Turner, apparently, was quite talented in that art form. But since the two of them were perched rather stiffly on the davenport as if waiting for an end to the preliminaries, he decided it would be wise to proceed quickly to the objective of his visit.

"The reason I asked to talk with you is that although you signed up for Pastor's Classes, you have missed the first two sessions, and I wondered if there was some problem . . . ." He let the sentence dangle and looked expectantly from one to the other.

Elizabeth, in turn, looked at Calvin. It was obviously up to him to answer. He leaned forward, elbows on his knees, and cleared his throat. "I'm not the kind of guy to beat around the bush. I believe in getting things right out in the open, minister or no minister." He paused as if expecting the pastor to say, "That's exactly the kind of

person I like to deal with!" The phrase that actually sur-
faced in Adam's mind was, *Man the battle stations!*

Hearing neither reaction, Turner continued forcefully,
"Frankly, I think all those classes are a waste of time. I
was a deacon and Sunday-school superintendent for
years, and the wife, here, has headed up the Women's
Missionary Society and taught Sunday school—all that
sort of thing. I simply don't think going through all that
beginner's stuff again is going to tell us anything we
don't know. Sure, a lot of people need it, but we're beyond all that."

"If you feel that way, why did you sign up?"

"Well! It became pretty obvious after all your an-
nouncements that anyone who expected to join would be
forced to. So I thought, 'Okay, we'll sign up, but we're
not going to sit through any more sessions than we have
to.' I mean, it gets boring, going over the same ground
again and again."

Adam had anticipated this as one of the possible reasons for the Turners' absences, but it intrigued him that
those who felt this way never seemed to realize what
their attitude revealed about them. Cal obviously looked
down on the others attending the classes as his spiritual
inferiors, though he knew none of them and had rejected
the possibility that the leaders might include in their
presentations something of worth for older Christians.
His former church offices were proffered as an official
badge to be flashed in order to gain immediate entry.

"Perhaps I could start by sharing with you what we,
the pastor and elders, see as the main value of the
classes," Adam replied. Cal leaned back on the couch,
his hands locked behind his head and legs extended.
Elizabeth's apprehensive demeanor remained un-
changed, though she was trying to act interested in what
Adam was saying. *Probably uneasy about Cal's blunt-*

ness, he thought, *and no wonder. His attitude has un-doubtedly alienated many potential friends.*

"There are several things we are trying to ac-complish," Adam went on. "Of course, we always in-clude a session on what it means to be a Christian—the basics you alluded to. Some need to start there, and we would be wrong if we didn't include the simple Gospel message in every phase of our church life, so no one can escape hearing it. But most of the ones who already un-derstand this part of things seem to feel like the line of the old hymn: 'Those who know it best seem hungering and thirsting to hear it like the rest.' "

He allowed time for this to sink in, then continued. "But there's so much more: learning what the church is, analyzing Christian maturity, sharing personal experi-ences in the Lord. Then we deal specifically with Cal-vary Church—our bylaws, budget, statement of faith.

"On top of all this is the opportunity to meet every church officer and his wife and to draw close to the other members of the group, so that if you join, you know at least a few people really well. Those are some of our goals, though I've probably left some out, too. So having stayed away twice, you have missed not only the lesson materials, but also an opportunity to meet some of the elders and deacons and to make friends with others in the class."

Cal sat up. "Well, to tell you the truth, I'm really not all that anxious to get buddy-buddy with anyone for a while. Of course, later, I'll probably be a church officer . . . ." Adam could not resist glancing at Elizabeth, who was biting on her upper lip and staring over her husband's head at the stitchery. ". . . but for now I want to stay uninvolved."

Adam smiled, and it was genuine, for the man's well-developed ego did amuse him. Cal didn't want to get close to people, just lead them. "Well, I'll tell you one thing, Cal. If you are contemplating a leadership position, every church officer has to be sold on the value of membership classes. They are the beginning commitment, the *first* step in a life of *continuing* faithfulness and dedication expected of each and every member."

Cal eyed him speculatively. "Then maybe Calvary Church isn't the place for me."

This statement was calculated to produce a frantic backpedalling on the minister's part, but failed in its objective. "That's exactly what you must determine *before* you join. One family came to all six weeks of instruction, heard us present the Gospel, listened to people telling them how to witness, found out about our calling program, signed a statement of faith, and joined. Three weeks later they wrote me and asked to be removed from membership, because we were too evangelistic for them. Now, what did they find out in those three weeks that they didn't discover in the two months before? I don't know. But we want to keep that kind of thing to a minimum. We know God isn't going to lead everyone to join Calvary Church. That's obvious. We want those who do become a part of us to be firmly convinced this is where God wants them to be."

The man was still appraising him, but there appeared to be less cockiness in the gaze. Cal, Adam thought, was the sort who tried to get everything on his own terms—membership, amount of participation, church office; the kind who would brag about how he "told him right to his face, minister or no minister." Time would tell whether he would pick up his credentials and go elsewhere.

Adam stood. "Well, Cal, Elizabeth, let me know what you decide, will you? If you will be coming to the remaining classes, I'll need to get you the materials you missed. If you want to wait until the next set of classes, that might be even better." He paused, but neither spoke. Cal was standing with his hands in his pockets and seemed to be considering something rather solemnly.

Adam continued, "I hope Calvary Church can be a home for you, but that must be your decision." He held out his hand, and Cal shook it readily. "Well, have a nice evening, you two. I hope I didn't delay your dinner too long."

The lessons still lay on the seat as Adam pulled away from the curb. He often could guess pretty well what the outcome of an encounter would be, but this one could go either way.

After collecting the boys from the neighbor's, Adam got the chicken and rice, milk, and some leftover gelatin salad on the table. The telephone rang while they were eating; it was Trudi.

"Chris is getting dressed. We're going to drive over to her parents in Hampton to pick up Doris and Ginnie."

"You are!" Adam was very surprised at this turn in events.

"Yes. Chris feels that maybe it will be bad for Ginnie to be gone any longer, that she might find it harder to face people, the longer it goes."

"I think she's right. I was concerned about that. You're going with her?"

"I'm driving. Chris wants me to go into the house with her, too. She wants Ginnie to see that we don't hold her responsible and that people can know what she's been through and not let it change their feelings toward her."

"That's quite a turnaround in her thinking!"

"You should see her. She's becoming so determined that Ginnie not suffer any more that she's a regular tiger!"

"What a relief! Has she talked about the Lord at all?"

"Yes. We decided that since He already knew about it, we could overcome our feelings of shame and talk to Him about it."

"You don't know how glad I am, honey. When I first got there I was afraid she had gone over the edge. I didn't feel like I was making any real contact with her until a few minutes before you arrived."

"That's what she indicated. She said you got her thinking about Ginnie's feelings, and she began to realize she had to do something besides sit around and cry."

"Well, don't worry about things here. I'm staying home; so the boys and I will watch a football game and take it easy."

"Good. I think Chris and I will stop for dinner on the way. She needs something to eat."

"Okay, honey, thanks a lot."

"Sure. See you later."

For some reason it was especially gratifying to have the boys around him that night. After their baths they settled, fuzzy pajamas and all, on top of him in his big chair. The warmth of their wiry bodies comforted him, as with one head on each of his shoulders, they watched, with only marginal interest, the two teams battling it out on television. *O Lord,* he prayed, *keep Tim and Matt safe from the wiles of the devil. Keep them innocent and undefiled. Heal Ginnie and Chris of their heartache. Help Ginnie not to fear and distrust all men or be permanently warped by this experience.*

He drew his arms more tightly about his sons. Maybe he'd let them stay up till Trudi got home if it wasn't too late. For the first evening since he could remember, the telephone did not ring, and he thanked a gracious Father for this time of peace and love.

4

Sanction the Unsanctified

"Remember, I won't be home 'for lunch today," Adam said sliding his tie into place.

"Oh, that's right! This is Thursday, your *Big Day!*" Trudi teased.

"Watch it, ma'am. Do not make fun of these solemn occasions. Your one and only is going to rub shoulders with the 'movers and shakers' today, and I demand a little more respect."

"Really, though." Trudi became more serious. "What are you going to say?"

"No problem. I am going to whip out my Prayer for Dedication of the New Fire Station, make a few skillful changes, and voilà, I will have one Prayer for Dedication of the New Freeway Interchange."

"I can't really see why they're making such a big deal about it."

"You are naive, my dear. It is an opportunity to have a noon blowout at the country club with the state picking up the tab."

"Oh. I hadn't thought of that."

Adam kissed her on the cheek. "That is why you will never get anywhere in this world, my dear. Those who *do* think of things like that."

"Is my lunch ready?" Tim was pulling a sweater over his head, ruining his freshly combed hair.

45

"It's on the sink along with your permission slip. Be sure to get it or you can't go on the trip to the bakery."

Matt's head popped through the door. "Is my lunch ready?"

Trudi laughed. "You two sound like those dolls with the pull-out rings on their tummies, repeating the same two or three phrases. How about, 'I lo-o-ove you, Mommy'?"

Matt's grin revealed several empty spaces. "I ain't no sissy doll!"

"You ain't no correct grammarian either. Who lets you talk like that?" Adam demanded.

"No one!" Trudi answered. "Kids who talk like that get thrown in the trash!"

Matt acted suitably dismayed at this long-standing threat and ran happily down the stairs to the kitchen. Trudi followed in order to make sure everything got sorted out properly and to see the boys out the front door.

"Have a good day, sweetie," she said to each of them. It occurred to her that perhaps this was not what one ought to call boys, but it felt right. If it ever started embarrassing them, she was sure she'd be the first to hear about it.

Adam was leaving, too. "And what's your schedule?" he asked, putting his arms around her.

"Get started on the housecleaning, so that no matter how many interruptions I have, I'll still get done by Saturday."

"What's Saturday?"

"The day the boys and their friends are around, and it's impossible to make any progress."

"Well, Mrs. Dunn, I will leave you to your fascinating and noble efforts."

"Have a nice freeway opening."

"If I ever say yes to another of these things, shoot me."

It was about one-fifteen when Trudi stopped, mop in hand, in the middle of the kitchen floor and listened. Was that sound she had heard Adam's car pulling into the garage? It couldn't be. He was lunching at the country club. A car door slammed. It certainly sounded like his! She leaned the mop against the refrigerator and started for the door that led into the garage. Before she reached it, Adam opened it and stepped in.

"Over already?" she asked in surprise.

"Hasn't even started, the lunch part, at least. Got something you can feed me?"

"Well, sure. What happened?" Trudi went to the pantry and got a can of soup.

Adam stopped at the doorway. "Is the floor wet?"

"I was just about done rinsing it. It should be dry around the table. Get a chair and come on in." She began heating the soup. "I'm sure you'd have gotten something better at the country club."

"Probably. But everyone except me has been drinking one after the other for an hour—also at the state's expense—and the conversation was getting unbearable." Adam settled himself at the end of the table. "Did you ever meet Pat Crenshaw?"

"Name's familiar, but I can't place her. Is she a member?"

"She was. We took her off the roll about a year ago. Hadn't been to church since anyone could remember. We tried several times to get into the home, but there was no interest whatsoever. Anyway, her husband was there today. He's supervisor for public works for the county. Well, about a half hour into the drinking session, he spotted me. He came over and started in about how you don't have to go to church to be a Christian, swearing a blue streak, and ended up calling me an s.o.b."

"Adam! What did you do?"

"Got red in the face, probably. I had heard he really blew a fuse when his wife got her letter of dismissal, so I guess the combination of seeing me and too much liquor set him off again."

"What happened then?"

"A couple of his friends came over and dragged him away. But a lot of people had begun to stare at me; so after a minute or two I decided to get out of there before lunch was served, and I was stuck for another hour."

"Oh, honey, I'm sorry. What a mess."

"It really was. I don't know why they even ask someone to come and pray. It's obvious they couldn't care less. They just endure it until you finally stop. It's like they think they need to patronize the ministers by letting them do their little thing so they won't get their feelings hurt. Never again!"

Trudi set the bowl of soup in front of him and went to get crackers and milk. "I know I feel that way a lot of times when they pray at sports events or political rallies. People are milling around, all excited about the game or whatever. Praying is the farthest thing from their minds."

"It's just as bad when you're not doing something 'official.' Unless it's a specifically Christian gathering, there are always some who have to prove that having a preacher around isn't going to cramp *their* style, and you eat lunch, listening to them taking the Lord's name in vain every ten seconds. That's the main reason I haven't joined a service club here. There is always a certain number of guys who have to prove what a man they are, and no matter how hard you try to avoid them, they end up sitting by you, swearing their heads off, or telling dirty stories."

Trudi stirred her coffee thoughtfully. "I remember a few men from the banquets we went to in L.A. I felt so sorry for the wives. Their husbands acted just like foul-mouthed high-school kids."

"I've never understood it. Lots of these guys hold really responsible positions. It's kind of scary to think that people so inadequate, or insecure, or needing attention, or whatever, are making decisions that affect people's lives. I can only pray that they are more in control and mature when they're flying that airplane or performing that operation or whatever else they do than they are most of the time I see them."

"I read about a judge who had drunk drivers videotaped and showed them the film when they were sober. It seemed to make quite an impression on them."

"I wonder. Would Crenshaw be embarrassed to see his encounter with me? It's hard to believe they don't really know what they're doing after a few drinks, but maybe they don't . . . ."

They sat in silence a minute or two. Then Adam hauled himself to his feet. "Well! Got to get back to the office."

"Honey, I'm sorry today was such a bomb."

"Oh, I ought to know by now it's the kind of thing you have to expect when you're the 'front man' for the church. I'll just have to take the advice I give everyone else and say, 'Praise the Lord.' " He smiled wanly. "See you about five-thirty," he said and left.

O Lord, bless Adam this afternoon, Trudi prayed. *You know he tries to do the right thing. This kind of experience, the humiliation and undeservedness of it, can get to you even when you don't want it to. Send someone or something special into his life today. Help him to sense Your closeness and love. Give him the assurance that*

You are accomplishing Your purpose through him to-day. For Jesus' sake, Amen.

For the meeting of the Sunday-school staff that evening, the pastor had been asked to give a talk on "Biblical Principles of Discipline." Adam knew it was a key topic, nevertheless he was finding it difficult to concentrate. When the phone intercom on his desk buzzed, he pushed the button. "Yes?"

"Liz Armstrong on line two," Sally reported.

Adam didn't especially feel like talking to anyone, but he pressed the square to the left. "Hi, Liz."

"Hi, Adam. Say, I was ironing just now and thinking about how much I've been receiving from your sermons lately, and I thought I'd just call you and tell you." Adam's eyes filled with tears, a very unusual occurrence. "I've been in a real spiritual rut lately," she went on, "but that sermon on the grace of God was such a blessing, I've practically been singing all week."

"Liz, you'll never know how much your call means. This has not been my favorite day."

"Well, I guess that's what the Lord had in mind, then. That's all. I'll let you get back to your work. I just wanted you to know that your ministry means a lot to Hal and me."

"As you two do to me. Thank you very much for troubling to call."

"No trouble. My pleasure! Bye."

Adam rested his forehead on his folded hands. *And thank You, Lord,* he prayed, *I really needed that.*

5

Provide the Social Amenities

When the telephone rang, Trudi was trying to combine whipped cream, beaten egg whites, and melted chocolate into a special dessert for a luncheon the next day and didn't dare stop. Steeling herself to endure the repeated clangor, she realized it no longer bothered her as much as it once had to let it go unheeded.

During the first months after Adam was called to his initial position as assistant pastor of a large church, she had responded immediately to every summons no matter how inconvenient. She felt guilty if she didn't catch it by the third ring. During her pregnancy this had been harder to accomplish, but she nevertheless answered the phone every time it rang, even when it interrupted a much-needed nap.

Then one day Trudi was bathing one-month-old Matthew when the telephone started in. She had read somewhere that if you had to leave a baby unattended, the safest thing to do was to wrap him securely and put him on the floor where he could not fall. She grabbed a large towel, folded it around Matt, laid him on his tummy on the bathroom rug, and dashed into the kitchen.

"Hello?" she gasped, out of breath.

"Hello. Is Reverend Dunn there, please?"

Trudi could not imagine why anyone expected to find a member of the staff at home at ten o'clock in the morning. "No, he isn't. Have you tried the church?"

"No, I haven't," the woman replied. "They're so busy down there, I just hate to bother them, so I thought I'd try you first."

That had changed Trudi's view about making unreasonable efforts to field every call, especially since that church employed two full-time secretaries.

Trudi poured the chocolate-cream mixture over chunks of angel-food cake and covered the pan with plastic wrap. The telephone began jangling again, and this time she answered it.

"Is Reverend Dunn there?" asked a woman with a quiet, precise voice.

Trudi glanced at the clock. It was eleven-fifteen. Surely Adam had not left to come home for lunch yet. "No, he isn't. Have you tried the church?"

"No, I haven't. But perhaps you could give me the information I need."

Trudi flipped a mental coin and chose: wedding. "I'll be glad to if I can."

"Could you tell me how many your church seats?"

Trudi smiled to herself. First things first. Get the essentials out of the way before we go on to minor details like whether or not the pastor feels he can marry people he has never seen before.

"It seats about five hundred."

"Oh, that's plenty large." There was something vaguely Oriental in her speech pattern. "And how large is your reception room?"

"We have one small one and the large fellowship hall. But I think you had better talk with my husband if it is a wedding you are inquiring about."

"Oh, this is fine. You are telling me what I want to know. Now, about how long is your husband's wedding service?"

"Well, actually, I guess it doesn't really last too long. But, you see, this is something you should discuss with him."

"Oh, I intend to do that. But if you would give me some additional information, I would appreciate it. Now would you say thirty minutes would be long enough for the ceremony?"

"I suppose so," Trudi answered, momentarily overcome by the woman's tenacity.

"And how much time, would you say, would elapse between the marriage service and the reception?"

Trudi tried to control her exasperation. "I'm sorry, but I have nothing to do with this sort of thing at all. You really will have to discuss the *possibility*," she emphasized the word, "of a wedding with my husband."

"I understand perfectly," the gentle, distinct voice continued unperturbed. "You see, we have certain problems we are trying to solve, and it will take only a few more minutes, and it will all work out fine, I am sure. It is my daughter who is to be married, and we, of course, want a church wedding. But her fiancé's parents are from the old country and will not enter a Christian church. So we are trying to see if we can arrange to have the reception start without the couple and have them go to his parents' home immediately after the church wedding for a Buddhist tea ceremony in order to satisfy his parents. Then the two of them can return and join the guests at the reception."

There was silence while Trudi tried to come to grips with the mental picture involved: Adam performing half of a Christian-Buddhist celebration.

The woman proceeded as businesslike as ever. "Do you happen to know if the church is already spoken for on Saturday, the twenty-fifth?"

Trudi realized this was usually the thinking of outsiders: The minister came with the church facility in sort of a package deal. If the building was available, then so, naturally, was the preacher.

"I'm afraid I neglected to get your name," Trudi countered.

"I am Mrs. Loo."

"Oh! I don't believe I have met you! Have you or your daughter attended our church?"

"No, but, of course, we expected to visit soon."

"Well, I have been suggesting that you call my husband before trying to work out all these details, because he has strong feelings about performing marriages. As a matter of fact, he rarely marries anyone who is not a church member. He believes that since he is paid by this particular group of people to be their pastor, counseling and performing marriages constitutes part of his pastoral function toward them. He feels he can honestly proclaim God's blessing on their marriage only if he knows that both of the couple believe in Jesus Christ and are committed to establishing a Christian home."

A second, more uncomfortable silence descended. When Mrs. Loo did not respond, Trudi went on, "So I really do think you should get in touch with my husband before you go any further in your planning."

"Yes, I will have to do that." Mrs. Loo's tone was still the essence of politeness and control. "You have been most helpful. Thank you for spending so much time with me."

"You're most welcome, of course." Trudi tried to match the other woman's courtly graciousness but felt decidedly inferior. "I hope we will meet soon."

"Thank you. Good-bye."

When Adam came home he had not heard from Mrs. Loo, but then neither of them expected he ever would. The twenty-fifth came and went without their detecting so much as a whiff of incense anywhere in town.

6

Keep Your Distance

Adam *had* to get a new suit. He kept about three in rotation at any given time, two to wear for good and one on its way out. But as he stood next to the couch where she was sitting while he read Scripture and prayed for the Lord's blessing on the Miller's new home, Trudi had seen from her vantage point that the specimen he was wearing was no longer "on its way out." It was gone! The thin spot on the seat was holding by two threads only. She had to struggle to keep from staring at those two fibers valiantly providing the slenderest of rear guards.

Trudi did not relish the prospect of finding a replacement for this threadbare item in his wardrobe. It wasn't only the money, though that was a consideration. They had learned long ago that it was false economy to buy a cheap suit; so an outfit that could take the constant wear Adam gave it would not be inexpensive. But the bigger strain would be hunting down the right one. Adam liked clothes but hated the process of acquiring them.

He insisted his wife go with him on such occasions, but seldom bought the one she liked best. He had definite ideas about what he wanted and recognized it when he saw it. Trudi had suggested he could do as well by himself, but he wouldn't hear of it; so she always ended up tagging along.

"That suit has had it," she announced when they arrived at home.

"It has?"

"It has. It's a good thing the jacket is as long as it is. Have you felt any unusual breezes from behind lately?"

Adam laughed. "Well, now that you mention it . . . no, not really."

"How much money do we have in the checking account?"

"About twenty or thirty dollars, I think."

"Any leeway when you get your next check?"

"I don't know. Maybe I can put off something."

"Well, when you take off that suit, give it to me, so you won't forget and wear it. I'll send the jacket to the mission, but those pants are totaled."

Four months had passed before Adam felt he could afford the clothes he needed. He had determined to use charge accounts only in cases of real emergency, and this was not in that category. He had charged the new tires he bought before driving a load of kids to camp, because the mechanic had told him the others were simply not safe. Physical safety was important enough to warrant using a credit card, but he got by with two suits until he could pay cash for a third.

Trudi had been on the lookout for sales and had been delighted to find that Harris and Frank's was having one, so now that the long-anticipated moment had arrived, they started looking there.

As soon as they entered the store, it dawned on Trudi why Adam needed her as an escort. *He* knew what clothes he liked, but *she* knew how to deal with salespeople. The odd fact was that this man, who was capable of coping daily with situations involving the whole range of the human predicament, faltered at the idea of facing a clothing-store employee alone. He who helped others come to terms with life at its most trying did not feel comfortable asserting himself as a buyer. This fellow who used such cutthroat tactics in Monopoly that she no longer would play the game with him (if he really loved her, would he put hotels on *all* his property?) could not tell a salesman no. In addition, she realized, Adam wanted someone on his side in the event that people found out he was a minister.

They had learned by painful experience never to divulge Adam's profession in a selling situation. People invariably felt uncomfortable in the presence of a "reverent." They usually had unshakable convictions about the type of clothing a "reverent" ought to wear. The Dunns had literally been driven out of stores by salesmen saying, "Here's a nice one, reverent. Now my wife's uncle—he's a reverent, too, and he always wears this style of shoe. Charlie, see if you have a ten D back there for the reverent!"

The store employee who waited on them proved to be especially proficient. He was friendly, witty at times, and knowledgeable. Conversation was confined to general topics, and when Adam had disappeared for the last time into the dressing room to remove the suit of his choice, Trudi thought they were home free. But then the salesman turned to her and asked, "And what line of work is your husband in?"

Trudi considered lying, but said instead, "He's a pastor," in a tone she hoped was neither apologetic, defensive, nor overly cheerful.

The man turned pale and seemed to shrink inside his clothes. He coughed nervously into his fist, then looked at Trudi with a miserable expression. "I hope I haven't said anything to offend you," he blurted, the strained look in his eyes revealing his efforts to recall every comment, every bit of banter that had passed between them.

"Not at all!" Trudi reassured him. "You've been most helpful." She smiled encouragingly.

Obviously unconvinced, he busied himself refiguring the totals on the sales slip.

After what seemed like a very long, quiet time, Adam emerged. The salesman led them as quickly as possible to the cashier's counter, practically bowing all the way, then made his escape.

Watching the man's retreating figure, while the girl processed his check, Adam muttered with an accusing undertone, "You told him!"

"I couldn't help it! He asked me flat out."

"He dropped us like a hot potato."

"Poor man. We scared him to death. He apologized for conversing with us as if we were normal people."

Adam smiled wryly and shook his head. "We'd better get out of here quick. If the cashier finds out what a weirdo I am, she might call off the whole deal."

7

Take Over
When I Take Off

Trudi had just begun to fill the tub for the boys' baths when the telephone rang. She shut off the water and rushed to answer it before it further disturbed the group gathered in the living room.

"Reverend Dunn, please," the male voice intoned.

"I'm sorry, but he's in a meeting. Could I take a message?"

"I need to talk to him right away. How soon will he be done?" The man was trying to mask his annoyance, but his manner still caused Trudi to bridle inwardly. She could tell he was not a member of the congregation; they understood when their pastor was not instantly available. It was the outsider that always wanted things *now*, *right away*. Hop to it, preacher. A stranger wants to spend part of your time for you. He has a need. How inconsiderate of you to be busy! You're supposed to be sitting by the phone waiting for his call.

Despite her emotions, Trudi kept her tone pleasantly businesslike, at least it seemed so to her. "I don't know how long the meeting will last. Probably for quite a while." Looking at her watch she saw it was only eighten-ten. "Could I take a message?" she repeated.

The man let out a couple of sighs while deciding. "No, I'll just call back later. Good-bye."

Trudi hung up and returned to the bathroom. The caller didn't even want to leave his name. Terrific!

The boys were playing like model children in their bedroom—an indication that they realized their bedtime was imminent. If they stayed quiet enough, she might forget about them. She turned on the water again, squirted in some liquid detergent, and proceeded to the boys' room.

As she reached the bedroom door, she halted abruptly and clasped both hands to her heart in mock emotion. "Oh, what darlin', beautiful little gentlemen," she gushed. "Just playin' so nicelike and quiet. I can hardly *stand* to interrupt! It don't seem fittin'!"

The boys looked up from the structure they were creating and grinned appreciatively.

"What a couple of phonies!" she laughed.

The spell broke, and Tim and Matt began wrestling and rolling around on the floor.

"Shh, shh!" Trudi moved to separate them. "Okay, don't fall apart. Your bathwater is ready so hurry up and get in there. I like your building."

"Batcave," Matt corrected.

"Okay, your batcave then." She looked for unusual winglike features but found none. "Tim, that's not where your shirt belongs!" she called, hurrying to shut off the almost-forgotten faucet.

The boys were drying themselves when the telephone's summons sent their mother trotting down the hall again.

"Hello?"

"Reverend Dunn, please." The same man again. Trudi's watch read eight-forty. Apparently she wasn't supposed to recognize him, so she played along. "He's in a meeting right now. Could I take a message?"

"Do you know when he'll be done?"

Really! she thought. "No, I don't."

The man paused uncertainly, emitting various sounds of irritation and indecision. After a few moments he said, "This is Darrell Mason. I've got to leave in a little while and need to talk to Reverend Dunn." There was another silence, and then he continued in a voice that sounded as if he were covering his mouth with his hand in order not to be heard by others at his end, "It's my wife . . . she's very upset, and I don't want to leave her this way."

The only Mason Trudi could think of was a young woman with a baby who had been attending church for a couple of months and who, if she remembered correctly, had said she had been having health problems ever since the baby was born.

"I really don't know what to tell you. When are you leaving?"

"Well . . . I don't plan to stay much longer . . . ."

Puzzled, she said, "Most of his meetings last until ten or so. Of course, if it's an emergency, I could interrupt . . . ."

Mason seemed to engage in another struggle with himself. "I don't know . . . it's *kind* of an emergency. I can't wait too much longer."

"Well . . . ." It was her turn to sigh. "I'll give him your message, but I can't guarantee he can get back to you right away."

"Tell him it's important, okay?"

"I will. What is your number there?"

He recited it to her and, with another comment or two stressing the seriousness of his circumstances, hung up.

Trudi went downstairs and stood just inside the entrance to the living room, waiting for a natural break in the proceedings. Adam and the Evangelism Committee were evaluating several methods and programs they had been involved with during the last two years, trying to decide which approaches fit Calvary Church's needs the best.

After a few moments Adam looked up. Trudi went over, and while the committee members waited, delivered in a low voice the message as succinctly as possible. Her husband screwed his mouth over to one side of his face as he deliberated. "Okay," he said, "I'll call him the first time there's a break."

The telephone rang again almost immediately, but this time it was the prayer chain. Trudi scribbled the message.

Oct. 15   Grace Smith   Healing
    Just received news of father's heart attack in Des Moines. Mother nearly blind. Pray as Spirit leads.

Twenty minutes later, though, it proved to be Darrell Mason again. Trudi felt it was no longer up to her to put him off. She went into the living room, and when Adam finished speaking and looked up, she shrugged and said, "It's that man again."

Adam rubbed his forehead. "All right. Ben, you and I discussed the statistics involved in this the other day. Why don't you go over those with the others while I try to find out what these phone calls are all about?"

Ben nodded and began looking through his stack of papers for the proper sheets. Adam went into the kitchen to take the call there, and his wife went upstairs and replaced the receiver on the bedroom extension.

In between her duties as telephone monitor, Trudi had managed to settle her sons into bed. Although it was now several minutes after nine and the movie she had contemplated watching was already in progress, she decided to tune it in anyway. Her husband's voice rumbled in the kitchen for some time, and she recognized in it a certain restrained quality that indicated the encounter was not an especially pleasant one.

Unable to concentrate on the TV program, Trudi switched it off when a particularly crass commercial came on and went downstairs to see if it would be possible to induce anyone to drink another cup of coffee. She wanted to make sure they knew it was decaffeinated. She couldn't stomach reheated coffee in the morning and over the years had undoubtedly thrown out enough of the brew to keep a ship afloat.

The meeting broke up at ten-thirty, and Trudi reappeared in time to tell everyone good-bye. Ben Tarrasa, the elder in charge of the Evangelism Committee, was the last to leave.

"I'm really pleased with the meeting," he said, his nearly bald head nodding in satisfaction. "I had hoped we could get the bulk of it done in one evening, and I think we did."

"You did an excellent job of keeping things moving, Ben. It's easy to get too involved sharing what happened on individual calls. You kept directing our attention instead to the overall impact of each program, and that's just what we needed."

"I think I'll have a recommendation ready for the next elders' meeting, so allow me a little extra time on the docket will you?"

Adam grinned. "You're the third one so far who's asked for 'a little extra time.'"

Ben laughed and shook his head. "We'll *never* have a 'normal' elders' meeting, I'm sure of it! Even when I get restless at how long they go, I can't see much we can leave out."

"Not without hampering communication. And when that goes, we're in trouble."

"Speaking of communication, I guess you got your telephone caller settled. I hope it wasn't too serious."

Adam snorted and looked disgusted. "Oh, it was serious enough. It was Janice Mason's husband. Have you met her?"

Ben shook his head no.

"She hasn't been attending too long . . . short brown hair and has a baby about six months old."

Ben still didn't remember her.

"Anyway, it was her husband, Darrell. It seems he's leaving her and going home to mama. For some strange reason this appears to have upset Janice, who hasn't been well anyway. And being of noble character, her husband didn't want to leave her in that state until he called me to inform me of the situation and ask me to help Janice in any way I can."

"How very thoughtful!" Trudi responded angrily. "Did you mention that you already have one wife to worry about?"

Ben stared. "That's incredible. What did you say?"

"I told him that even though she wasn't a member, we would, as a church, naturally do what we could for her; but what she needed most was a husband, and that was his responsibility. Calling me didn't change that."

"What did he say to that?"

"Oh, nothing much. Just that he couldn't take the pressure anymore and so on. I told him in that case *he* was the one who needed the help, and he should be calling me for himself and not for her. He said he didn't want any help; he just wanted out. I told him that God still held him responsible for his wife and that no running away would change that. From then on we just went over the same ground. I have no doubt he left as soon as he hung up."

"Beautiful!" Trudi broke in. "Just call up the pastor and turn your wife over to him. People are insane! Here's a guy who bothers *me* three times, insists on interrupting a meeting to talk to *my* husband fast, because he's 'got to leave soon,' so he can put *my* husband in charge of *his* wife! A nice trick if you can pull it off!"

"I know, honey, I know." Adam put an arm around her and pulled her closer. He felt all the vexation she did— all the disgust and indignation at the immaturity and irresponsibility of so many, especially men. Husbands were far worse than wives when it came either to infidelity or instigating separation, at least in his experience. Never mind the vows, forget the promises, ignore the people counting on you, just bail out when things get tight and leave your job to someone else.

Ben shifted his stack of folders and papers to his other arm and sighed. "She's not a member; so she hasn't been assigned to one of the undershepherds, has she? Is she a Christian?"

"I'm not sure. I called on her and didn't get any indication that she wasn't. Has she had an evangelism call yet? I haven't received any report of one."

"I'll check. Well, the meeting went well, anyway," he reminded them.

Adam nodded and smiled. "If I could spend all my time with you guys, I'd have it made."

"Well, good night, you two. Try to forget the Mason mess and get a good night's rest, will you?"

"Oh, we will," said Trudi, somewhat mollified.

"Thanks, Ben, we will," Adam echoed and saw Ben out the door.

Trudi went into the kitchen and dumped the rest of the coffee down the drain. Adam entered, carrying a couple of forgotten cups and napkins.

"Adam Dunn," Trudi intoned, "Surrogate Husband of the World!"

"Gertrude!" Adam remonstrated. "You shouldn't say that! Do you know what an awful connotation that has?"

"I guess so, now that you mention it."

"Well, don't ever say that to anyone else!"

"I won't. I just wanted to get it all out of my system."

"You know, you're terrible," he said, putting his arms around her and kissing her in such a way that she didn't feel terrible at all.

8

Keep Wheels and Palms Greased

Adam contemplated the stack of papers on his desk with something less than jubilation. Although very much aware that each sheet represented a vitally important issue in some person's life, he chafed under the burden of trying to produce carefully considered, honest opinions and the drudgery of continuously filling out forms. "The ministry" was not at all like most people thought it was, he mused. His own seminary-inspired visions of hours of uninterrupted study and finely honed sermons seemed naive. Real life was neither so predictable nor so tidy as youthful idealism imagined it.

The easiest items to dispose of lay at the top of the pile. Two young people had submitted his name as a reference when applying for jobs. He knew one of them well; the other he had never heard of. The next sheet requested his opinion of a college girl who was competing for a scholarship for a year's study in Europe. The one below that was an inquiry regarding the suitability of one of Calvary's members for a teaching position in a Christian school. The bottom three-page form came from the county agency to whom the Templars had applied in order to adopt a child. Adam had arranged the sheets in the order of their importance: those concerning money and position could be dispensed with after a minimum of soul-searching; the inquiries having to do with human lives, especially those of children, would demand a greater expenditure of time.

The applications concerning the job for the teenager with whom he was acquainted and the collegian hoping for a trip to Europe were completed when a light knock sounded, and Sally stepped in carrying the day's mail.

"I was just going to buzz you, Sally." He stood up and handed her the reference request from the unknown young person. "Would you contact the high-school-group sponsors and Sunday-school teachers and see if they know this Kevin Hartley?"

Sally nodded. "Sure. The name doesn't ring a bell with me." Larry Jacobs, Sally's eighteen-year-old son, was a leader in the high-school group, which kept her in contact with most of the boys involved in the church's programs.

"Not with me, either. Tell them I'll accept their opinion if he has come often enough for them to have a reasonably accurate opinion of his character, but that they shouldn't go out on a limb if he just drops in occasionally. If none of them know him well, I'll send it back with a 'does not attend regularly enough to evaluate' on it. That should tell them quite a bit."

"At least it ought to make them wonder why he would put you down for a reference."

"Right." He perused the stack of mail Sally had laid on his desk. The letters addressed to the church had been opened and sorted; the ones directed to him personally had been left sealed.

"Well," he commented appreciatively, "I see some of the membership class actually mailed in their applications immediately, just as I asked them! I'm going to have to put gold stars on their certificates."

Sally grinned. "You must have really scared them. This is only Friday, and you have four returns already! Oops, there's the phone!" She hurried out.

Adam sat down and flipped through the first of the membership applications. He had not reminded himself to gird his loins for this week's encounters, so he had better prepare himself mentally now. Over the years he had reached the conclusion that people could sit through any number of weeks' instruction and still not come to grips with whatever their own particular problem was until it came to signing on the dotted line. Some even arrived at the final session, uncompleted application blank in hand, waiting for the deciding factor that would make up their minds for them. Adam would receive disturbed and disturbing calls all week. He would lose sleep worrying about the theological issues, complaints, and uncertainties that would inevitably surface within the next few days. The only thing he could do to ease the tension ahead was to remember that the syndrome was as predictable as it was unavoidable.

Adam picked up a particularly fat envelope, still sealed because it was addressed to him, and slit it open carefully, leaving the stamp unharmed for one of his boys' collections. He removed a sheaf of papers, which proved to be a three-page typewritten letter and two blank membership forms. The letter was signed by Calvin and Elizabeth Turner.

Adam had been surprised when the Turners showed up for the third session of the Pastor's Class and attended the next two as well. They had not "let him know of their decision" as he had asked them to do, but he had overlooked that and given them the back materials on the first night they attended. Cal had been outgoing—even hearty—in his contacts with the other class members and warm toward the elders and deacons. The contents of the envelope, however, showed that these positive indications had not come to flower. Adam settled back in his chair and read.

Dear Pastor Dunn:

As you know, we began attending the membership classes with reservations and much reluctance. It was our view that meetings of that type would not be of much benefit to us at our stage in Christian life. After your visit to us, we felt obligated to attend, and our above-mentioned beliefs were confirmed. We already know about Bible study, prayer, stewardship, etc., and we continue to be upset by being forced to spend three evenings attending classes.

We were surprised to learn from the evening spent studying the bylaws of Calvary Church that the elders are also trustees. It would be far better to have two separate boards, one to handle the spiritual matters of the church, while the other takes care of the business matters. This way more people are in positions of leadership and each decision can have more input from more points of view. Also, there are many men who have fine business sense but do not see themselves as being "spiritual." A board of trustees would provide a place for these people to serve in the church.

Adam thought he could guess who Cal Turner might have in mind as a member of one of the expanded boards.

As a matter of fact, we were disappointed with the attitude of the elders we did meet. I have worked on many boards in the past and do not believe that their show of perfect harmony was sincere. Also, it is natural that the leaders should present Calvary Church in the best possible light, but they did not act as if they saw any faults in the church at all. I can assure you there are some things that could be improved. In short, the elders and deacons seem to have formed a clique which keeps others out of places of leadership and which discourages suggestions for improving Calvary Church.

Last, we thought some of the items on the membership application were ridiculous. What possible need could there be for asking for the wife's maiden name? It also seems to us to be improper to request people to list churches where they were members previously. That should have nothing to do with the present situation. There are boxes to check to tell whether or not we have been baptized! How in the world could anyone join a church without being baptized? There are spaces to list names of children, showing insensitivity toward those without children. The whole application seemed to us to be an affront to our personal dignity.

We have therefore returned the applications to you. We realize that, the way things are run there, this probably will mean we will not be allowed to join. Therefore we will not attend the final class session.

Sincerely,
Calvin and Elizabeth Turner

P.S. We enjoy the fellowship of the members of the church and will continue to attend unless further irritations arise.

Adam tossed the letter onto his desk and tipped further back in his chair. He wanted to laugh at the dis-

play of pique contained in the three pages, but he was
too provoked himself to do it. Turner undoubtedly considered himself to be the one to whom the elders should
flock in order to be enlightened about ways to improve
the church, but it would be a cold day in July . . . . He
sat up and put the letter in one of the in-out trays to be
dealt with when he was in a more conciliatory mood.

Adam composed a positive recommendation for Lily
Vasquez to teach at the South Side Christian Day School.
Looking at his watch, he saw what his stomach had been
indicating for quite a while—it was past time for lunch.
When he reached the outer office, he found that Sally
had already gone for her noon break; so he laid the form
about Lily on her desk to be typed up when she returned
and went home.

Upon returning to the church office, Adam found that
Sally had company. The old man with the stringy gray
hair and beard, greasy black jacket, and filthy blue pants
who was holding forth—no doubt for a handout—was
Old John, the resident bum and local landmark. No one
seemed to know where the man lived, but he could usually be found either rummaging through someone's trash
cans or standing out on the edge of town, waving a welcome to cars as they entered on the main highway. This
was a surprising visit, for there was no new personnel at
Calvary Church. Old John, who had a nose for such
things, normally hit churches only when an unsuspect-
ing new pastor had just begun his duties. He even kept
track of the arrivals of assistant pastors and youth direc-
tors, and from time to time tried his hand with one of
them.

Sally looked relieved to see Adam swing through the
door, and Old John turned and favored the new arrival
with a wide toothless grin.

"Well, hello, O.J.," Adam greeted him. "What are you doing here?"

John ignored the question and held up one leg, displaying a paint-spattered, badly scuffed black shoe which had cord wound around and around the toe in an effort to keep body and sole together. "How do you like my shoes?" he crowed.

"I think you need some new ones."

"*New ones!* These *are* new! Got 'em just last week. My other ones finally wore out."

Adam smiled and shook his head. "I guess your taste in clothes and mine just don't jibe. What are you doing here?" he repeated. "You know you go either to the mission or the Salvation Army if you need a meal."

Old John nodded heartily. "I know that."

Just then Adam spotted the dog on its leash, the bullterrier of indifferent lineage that was its owner's constant companion. "John, you know we don't want animals here in the office. Get to the point."

The dog, responding to the less friendly intonation in Adam's voice, hoisted its overfed bulk to its feet and stood wheezing at him in a menacing manner. The derelict's characteristic odor, resembling that found under the hood of an overheated automobile, filled the room. Sally rolled her typing table and chair as far away as possible and began working engrossedly.

"I just wanted a little money for a present. Today's Dolly's birthday." He gestured toward the emphysematous pet, and Adam noticed for the first time a huge red bow dangling beneath its jowls. John stooped and slid the ribbon up along the collar until it rested on the spot perhaps called the back of the neck. The effect was rather like tying a lace cap on a gorilla. Adam controlled a shudder and looked away. "And how old is Dolly?" he asked.

Old John's eyes crinkled as he displayed a marvelous expanse of gums. "I'm not rightly sure."

"How many 'birthdays' has she had so far this year?"

"Now, Reverend Dunn. What kind of question is that? You don't think I'd try to put one over on you, do you?"

"I don't 'think'; I *know!*" Adam eyed him speculatively for a few moments while the old man bent down and patted Dolly with a gnarled hand. "Do you keep your promises?" he asked suddenly.

Old John's face registered surprise at the question, and then gave way to a crafty expression as he straightened himself up and looked at his questioner. "I don't *make* many promises," he said.

Each continued to take the other's measure with his gaze. Finally Adam said, "I'll give you a dollar for Dolly's birthday—or whatever else you want to spend it on—if you'll *promise* me you won't spend it on liquor."

Old John met his eyes steadily. "I'm a no-good bum, but I ain't no wino," he snapped.

Adam got out his wallet. "Is that a promise?"

John shuffled uneasily from one foot to the other. Giving his word apparently *was* a painful process. The vagrant sighed heavily. "Yeah, it's a promise," he said at last and took the bill held out to him.

Adam grinned. "This is November, so don't come around with this birthday pitch for a full year. You know, everyone says you're the richest man in town, anyway."

"Do they now?" Old John looked at him with a sly smile as he jammed the dollar into his grimy trousers' pocket. He clucked a sound at Dolly, who started forward. "Do they now?" he repeated, and chuckled to himself as he led her, rasping with every breath, out into the corridor and through the outer door to the sidewalk.

Adam looked sheepishly at his secretary. "Guess I'm getting soft in the head."

She shook her head in disbelief. "I think so!"

"I was either overcome by the smell, or I'm just tired of telling everyone no. It's kind of neat to be a nice guy for a change."

Sally was still shaking her head as he turned to go into the office.

"You'd better open the windows, even if we freeze," he called. "I'd hate for anyone coming in here to hold one of us responsible for these fumes."

9

Be Wise as Serpents, Harmless as Doves

The adoption papers for Anne and Darren Templar presented the pastor with a dilemma. The couple had been on the brink of separation twice within the last three years—the most recent, according to his notes on their card, a year ago. Could he honestly recommend placing a child in such a potentially unstable situation? Adam was stuck mentally reviewing over and over again the different aspects of the problem when he decided to buzz Sally.

"Yes?"

"Sally, say something cheerful. I don't think I've heard one happy sound all day."

"The mimeograph machine isn't working."

"Thanks a lot. If your children asked for bread, you'd give them a stone, wouldn't you?"

Sally reflected upon the accusation. "Only," she decided, "if the oven worked as badly as our mimeograph."

Adam laughed, switched off the intercom and looked at the Templar's adoption papers. It hit him forcefully that there was no way he could, in good conscience, recommend them as parents. Anne and Darren were dealing with each other on a very immature level, and their marriage was a contest of wills. Perhaps a child would redirect their goals, but it was not a risk he personally would be willing to advocate. Although the two of them had recently become part of one of the small study groups in the church, it was too early to tell whether they would be able to let Christ rebuild their relationship. But how to reply to the agency's request without ruining the couple's chances for a family in the future if they should get their attitudes straightened out . . . .

Adam decided to leave the form in his in-out tray as long as possible, even though the unfinished project would nag him for as long as it lay there. He had always suspected that no one paid much attention to his efforts on such documents, anyway—a notion emphasized by the fact that he had received one such form after the baby was already in the adoptive home! If some official called to inquire about his delay, he could decide then. What he most wanted was more time for the Templars to work out things and this was the only way he could think of to get it.

The chairman of the prayer chain called to inform him that Sarah Raymond had been admitted to the respiratory-ailment section of the Eastland Community Hospital with an acute case of asthma. Also, Doris Tacher's biopsy had been malignant, and a hysterectomy was scheduled for the following day. The prayer group, one of the most active sets of volunteers in the church, handled requests involving a wide range of need throughout the community, but only those pertaining to members of Calvary's congregation were passed on to its pastor.

Adam could visit Sarah tomorrow, but he should drop in on Doris this afternoon since the suddenness and seriousness of her surgery might have caught her emotionally and spiritually unprepared.

Pulling the Turners' epistle toward him, Adam waded through its contents again. Did it demand a response, or should he let the matter drop? Experience warned him he would get into trouble either way. It would either be, "We wrote a three-page letter and were not even treated to the courtesy of a reply," or "His cold, unloving letter was the last straw." If he was going to send it, he wanted to get it over with; otherwise he'd be composing letters all night. Besides, tomorrow others in the membership class would no doubt present him with additional problems to contend with.

He remembered one couple who had attended classes after reportedly being led to the Lord by a neighbor. They had many problems, and he had spent time in their home, trying to help them work things out. It wasn't until the membership classes were well under way that they revealed to him that they weren't married, that each had a spouse who was also living unmarried with someone else, and that one of the children was hers, while the younger child had been born to them after they began living together.

Attempting to discern Christ's answer to such an alliance had not been easy. In the end, after several soul-wrenching sessions, the pastor's conclusions had been unpalatable to the couple, and they had dropped out of sight. This was another pain stored in Adam's memory which, along with its accompanying sense of failure, got stirred up from time to time.

Reaching into a drawer, Adam removed several pieces of scratch paper—the recalcitrant mimeograph machine was his continuing source of supply—and set to work trying to frame a suitable answer for the Turners. After several attempts, he arrived at a version that served his purpose. Pulling out his own typewriter and a package of erasable bond—he preferred not to include Sally in these situations—Adam copied his handwritten response.

Dear Cal and Elizabeth,

I was very sorry to receive your letter and learn that attending the Pastor's Classes was such a disagreeable experience for you. We sometimes find individuals who at first would prefer not to come to the classes, but almost all of these feel differently before the sessions conclude. I regret that this was not true in your case.

You have raised several issues which I feel should not be left without clarification on our part. You favor having the trustees comprise a board separate from the elders. I realize this is done in some churches. However, we believe that every decision, financial or otherwise, is a spiritual one. Those who make decisions regarding the programs of the church must also be free to appropriate the money to fund those programs. God uses mightily those who have financial acumen in the Body of Christ when they are spiritually sensitive to His will. There is no greater need for spiritual insight than among those who must decide how best to use the tithes and offerings of God's people.

I am surprised and saddened that you perceived the spirit of joy and unity demonstrated by the elders to be insincere. I can only say that while the men come from varied backgrounds and have differing opinions from time to time, they share a common wholehearted commitment to the work of the Lord which has created a genuine love among them for each other. They have worked hard to let no root of bitterness spring up among them, to speak the truth in love, and to esteem others more highly than themselves according to the biblical injunctions.

Calvary Church, despite our efforts, is not all it could be. This is true because no one, neither I, as pastor, nor any member, is all that he should be. We hope you will pray for the lacks you see in our fellowship and ask the Lord to form us more perfectly into His likeness.

With regard to the membership application blank, without replying item by item, I would merely point out that most questions are motivated by a desire to get to know each member more personally. In addition, churches receive occasional requests for recommendations or information to be used for legal purposes, such as establishing date of birth. It is helpful to have some basic data on hand to avoid confusion.

I hope this letter has helped to explain some of the items troubling you. I also hope that "further irritations" do not arise. If they should, I trust you will continue to resolve them in the biblical manner, sharing them only with those involved either in the problem or its solution.

Unless I hear from you to the contrary, I plan to read your letter and this reply to the elders at our next meeting so that they may be apprised of your views.

It is my hope that Calvary Church can minister to both of you. May God bless you as you endeavor to find your church home.

Sincerely in Christ,
Adam Dunn
Pastor

Adam addressed the envelope, inserted the letter, and sealed it. When leaving to visit Doris, he would drop it on Sally's desk to be sent out with the rest of the day's mail.

He pulled Doris Tacher's card out of his file. She and Dave had three children, ages two to seven.

O Lord, Adam prayed, *cure Doris of her disease. Guide the surgeon tomorrow and give him Your wisdom. Give me Your words of comfort and hope as I go to see her now. Amen.*

He picked up the Turners' letter, went out of his office door, and locked it.

"I'm going to the hospital, and then home," he told Sally. "Have you called the mimeograph repairman?"

"Yes, but of course he can't get out today. At least I got the Sunday bulletin done yesterday. The stuff I was doing can wait till Monday."

"Good. Take it easy tomorrow," he said. Saturday would be her day off, but not his. Mondays still worked best for him, though he tried to spend Saturday afternoons with Matt and Tim when he could.

"I will, as much as I can. Larry has a preseason basketball game that Dan doesn't want to miss. It's not exactly restful, but it's fun. And I might even get out of cooking dinner!" She paused, carefully rearranging the pencils on her desk. "What do you think about Doris?"

"I don't know. If they caught it as early as it sounds as if they did, then the likelihood of the cancer's spreading seems pretty small. I tell you, the bill for Trudi's yearly checkup is probably the one I pay the most cheerfully of them all. I can't think of any better way to spend money than that."

Sally nodded. "Well, tell Doris we're all praying for her."

"I will. See you Sunday, and tell Larry I hope he runs the other team off the court."

Sally laughed. "Okay. If yelling will do any good, Dan and I will see to it. But then, Larry doesn't need much encouragement. If only he would put just a fraction of that energy into keeping his room decent . . . ." She shook her head and returned to her letter writing until Adam had gone. Then she stopped, and with tears welling in her eyes, asked the Lord to restore Doris to complete health so that she might also have the privilege, the special joy, of watching her own son grow into young manhood.

10

Stay in Good
With Other Christians

Adam forced himself to attend the local ministerial-association meetings. He was sure it was a flaw in his character, but he was not a groupthink person. He had come to feel, after years of participation in such groups, that they accomplished little of value in the areas he considered most important. Each congregation represented had its own ideas of how best to worship, evangelize, feed the hungry. Their pastors had by now acquired firm convictions regarding the various areas of Christian endeavor and no amount of discussion, it seemed to him, would produce anything more than a friendly agreement to disagree, and often even that was strained.

Heading a committee to organize a combined community Thanksgiving service held no interest for Pastor Dunn, but he had been assigned that job. He did not even care if there was such a gathering. The members of Calvary Church had never displayed much interest in communitywide services, either. They expected a sermon to contain some scriptural meat, and too often the pulpit offerings on such occasions were long on platitudes and generalities, and short on "thus saith the

Lord." The members enthusiastically supported inter-
denominational Bible studies or evangelistic efforts, but
services observing a particular day found few from his
congregation in attendance.

Adam had devised a plan for getting a good crowd,
including Calvary Church people, out to the service: an
interchurch children's choir would be singing. The
elementary-school-age choirs in each church had been
sent the music, and the reports were that, despite the
number leaving town for the holiday, at least one
hundred children—and their parents and grandpar-
ents—would show up on Wednesday evening. He was a
little uncomfortable with this method of pumping up the
attendance. They didn't use gimmicks to attract a congregation at Calvary Church, and it offended his
straightforward nature to "work an angle" for any reason.
But he also detested having something fizzle if he was in
charge of it, and the natural desire for the approval of his
colleagues in ministry was a powerful inducement for
courting success.

The ministerial-association meeting was at the
Methodist Church this month; the Ladies' Aid Society,
no doubt, had been persuaded to cook the one-dollar-a-
plate luncheon. Few cars graced the parking lot when
Adam arrived. Pastors were, if anything, even worse than
laymen when it came to being on time for meetings. No
one seemed to realize that it reflected a poor opinion of
another person if his time was considered less valuable
than your own, and he was kept waiting while you attended to more important matters.

Adam braced himself for his role as a buffer between
the groups of clergymen residing at the opposite ends of
the theological spectrum. He considered himself a "con-
servative" and an "evangelical" but was not comfortable
with the "fundamentalist" label even though he cer-

tainly believed in the "fundamentals" originally associated with that term. He was not theologically liberal, but did, on the other hand, stress reaching out to the poor and hungry more than some of those whose biblical views were closest to his own. He desired, along with the liberals, to see Christians more active in social and political arenas, but disagreed with their insistence that there be "no strings attached" to the physical and monetary help given. On the contrary, he believed that every cup of cold water and prison visit should be clearly identified as being "in Jesus' name" so that the true motivation for the act would be unmistakable. As a result, he often felt himself to be in an ideological "no man's land" with cross fire whistling past him from both sides.

Peter Driscoll was the first minister to greet Adam as he entered. Adam's olfactory senses reported that tuna casserole and carrot salad were almost certainly the day's menu.

"Hello, Pete, how're you doing?"

"Okay, I guess."

"That's hardly a ringing affirmation of well-being," Adam laughed.

"I just got through with a difficult conversation with one of my church officers." Pete shook his head wearily. "I've told them not to get mixed up in these crusades, but nothing doing. They got a whole bunch to drive over to Eastland last week, and now he's claiming he 'accepted Christ' over there and has got all these ideas of about fifty things we need to change. Good night! He's been a church officer for twenty years and thought everything was fine." He sighed. "It'll take me months to get his head screwed back on right."

Adam prayed for the right response. "What kind of changes is he suggesting?" They moved to the coffee urn and filled two Styrofoam cups.

"Oh, the same ones they all do after these things. More Bible studies, trying to get a busload of teenagers to go to Eastland for the final meeting . . . ." He snorted. "*That's* all I need. Get a bunch of emotional kids all fouled up, and their parents will be on the phone all week."

Some of the Calvary Church's high schoolers were attending the Saturday-night rally, but Adam felt it would be wiser not to mention that. Instead he said, "Pete, you know, it is possible to hang around the church for a long time because you know it's a worthwhile organization, and good for the community and all, without ever personally recognizing Jesus in your own life. I often have people tell me they 'played church' for years without letting it touch their hearts."

Driscoll eyed him suspiciously. "You sound like one of 'them'! "

"Well, in a way, I am. Not everyone can point to one day when they became a Christian, but that's the way it happened to me many years ago. So perhaps I can understand your man's feelings. Let's face it, Pete. All of us pastors get caught in the routine and become worn down spiritually from time to time." Adam fervently prayed he wouldn't say the wrong thing. "Sometimes it *is* hard to handle it when people go off somewhere, get all fired up, and drop it all on us at once." Pete was studying his coffee. "But the guy must have a lot of love and respect for you if he is willing to share something so personally important with you." He gave a short laugh. "You know, pastors can't do all the pushing and pulling. Your layman's enthusiasm may be just what you need right now."

Pete shook his head doubtfully. "I don't know. I think it's going to be a problem. I just don't understand the kind of language he's using now. He's not the same guy he was."

Adam was trying to frame a reply when a hand grabbed his upper arm and gave it a painful squeeze. Adam turned to see Howard Blankenship's ruddy face beaming at him.

"Good to see you, brother!" Howard effused.

"It's good to see you, too, Howard," Adam replied. "How are things going?"

"Oh, we're preaching Christ and upholding His word, and the Lord is just blessing mightily!"

Adam saw Pete begin to move away, a disgusted expression on his face, but Howard did not seem to notice. Adam didn't much blame Pete. He, too, felt preached at, and that made his answering smile a forced and inadequate reflection of the joy-filled countenance facing him. "Well," he replied, "I guess if we weren't doing that, we should get out of this business, shouldn't we?"

Howard looked somewhat taken aback, and then recovered with a hearty slap on the back. "That's right, that's right. Pra-a-aise the Lord!" he said loudly, then left to go across the room to greet someone else.

Adam sipped his coffee, momentarily alone. It was going to be a long afternoon. He could feel it.

One of the proposals brought up during the session was that of a pulpit exchange, with each minister trading with another so that congregations could get to know other pastors in the area. The pros and cons of this venture were tossed around for some time, and finally a list of tentative assignments was made up by the secretary. Changes could be made, but the secretary would have to be notified.

When the meeting had concluded, Adam went up to the front to check out his partner. He found he was to swap with Craig Jamison, pastor of one of the newer fellowships in town. He walked over to the cluster of men which included Jamison, and at a break in the conversation drew him aside.

"I see you and I are listed together. Do you think it will work out?"

The younger man looked at Adam seriously. "I hate to say so, but I don't think it would be a good idea."

Adam's eyebrows went up. "Oh? How come?"

Craig looked uncomfortable. "Well, Adam, my lay leader seems to have something against you, and since our group is pretty small . . . ."

"Something against *me*? What?"

"Well, it seems his family used to be in your church, and he feels you weren't as helpful about a family problem as they had hoped you would be."

"Who is it?"

"Ed Elkins."

"Ed Elkins! So that's where they went. His deacon tried to get into the home, but they just told him they were attending elsewhere; so we took them off the rolls." Adam digested the new insights. "So he's upset, because I didn't solve his family's problems, huh? Did he mention what those problems were?"

The other minister shook his head.

"Well, now, that's real sweet. They go around giving me a bad name while I'm supposed to keep all their messes a secret. Well, I'll tell you what they were. Neither of them wanted to go to the trouble of taking time off from work to drive their son to a hearing about some drug charges; so they asked me to do it. I spent a lot of time with them and did a lot of other stuff for them, like visiting the boy in jail. If they're telling people I ignored them, that's really hard to take."

". . . Perhaps I'd better have a talk with them . . . ."

Adam took a deep breath and let it out slowly. "No, Craig, don't bother. It won't do any good to open old wounds. I find this all the time. The people who demand the most from you are the ones who will turn on you the quickest. It's as if they think they will expunge all the bad experiences they've involved you in by blotting you out of their lives."

Jamison seemed at a loss for words. Adam guessed that was partly caused by his new perspective on his lay leader—questions that gave one pause. Finally he asked, "What do you think we should do about the pulpit exchange?"

"Oh, let's forget it. I'm not one for that kind of thing, anyway." Adam smiled wryly. "If we don't make a fuss, maybe none of the others in the association will notice."

"I'm really sorry about all this," Jamison said uncertainly. "I guess I shouldn't have said anything."

"Oh, no. I was bound to hear about it sooner or later. Don't worry about it. Maybe if you keep preaching at him, he'll have a change of heart and come to love me like a brother."

Craig smiled for the first time since their conversation began and was about to say something more when Howard Blankenship bore down upon them. "I'm leaving now," he announced. "I just wanted to say 'Lord bless ya' before I went. Have a great week, you two."

"Thanks, we will," they answered in unison, but Adam didn't know how in the world his week could ever be as great as Howard's apparently always were.

As he drove back to the church, Adam prayed. *Lord, is all this really what being in the ministry is all about? Is this worth my life? What does any of this accomplish? I've used up a whole day on this. Did it mean anything?*

He waited for an answer. No new insights or blinding revelations came, but instead a sort of inward soothing, as if a layer of calmness was flowing over all his exposed nerve endings and hurt feelings, cooling and comforting them.

Okay, Lord, I'll keep hacking away if You say so. You're the boss, and You can use me any way You want to. But if You come up with some more rewarding ways to spend my time, I'd like You to let me know about them as soon as possible.

11

Don't Let Things
Get You Down

Sprawled idly in his big easy chair, the pastor of Calvary Church was feeling rather pleased with himself. For the first Christmas he could remember, they were ahead of the game. He stretched his feet as close to the fire as he dared and ticked off the completed responsibilities in his mind: outdoor lights up, Christmas letters mailed, tree selected and decorated, shopping for Trudi's presents completed. He had even finished assembling Tim's new bike just a few minutes ago and would not have that sort of chore waiting for him, as had sometimes been the case, when they got home from the Christmas Eve communion service. A satisfied glow enveloped him as he sat slouched just watching the leaping flames and holding the Christmas cards Trudi had handed him.

When he finally roused himself enough to look through the new batch of greetings, they proved to be representative of the many they had already received. The first ones were from members of the congregation and many of these contained notes of appreciation for various blessings received through Adam's ministry or problems surmounted with his help during the year. These were a great encouragement to the pastor's heart and made him feel that his efforts, after all, were bearing some sort of fruit.

It was somehow much easier for Adam to accept praise or expressions of gratitude in written form than face to face. He tended to withdraw somewhat when people tried to verbalize approval even though he really believed people needed to express these positive emotions, and to learn to receive them as well.

That was one of the problems with being in the Lord's work. If things were going well and spiritual growth was evident, then the praise and glory, of course, belonged to God. He was the One who deserved the credit if a sermon was a blessing, even if the preacher had spent three solid days on it—everyone knew that—which made it difficult for the minister to know how to respond to favorable comments without sounding stuffy.

Adam had a sneaking suspicion that God meant for all men in His will, including pastors, to take healthy pride in their day's work. But when the Lord has said, "*I* will build my church," it would seem dangerous to allow yourself to be proud that your congregation has doubled in the last five years, even if other groups in town haven't. The fear that you might be judged for accepting praise that belongs to God alone appeared to be a valid one. You could possibly swell with pride at doing an especially fine job as an engineer or carpenter or salesman. But as a pastor? It would somehow be out of place.

Adam sighed. He was sure the Lord had a right sort of satisfaction reserved for His full-time servants, but he was having a hard time getting a grasp on it. At any rate, the private notes in his hand, and others like them over the years, probably contained the greatest personal reward he cared to receive.

He turned his attention back to the remaining cards and letters. Most of these were from friends from seminary days, and while it was pleasant to catch up with their news, there were heartaches to be shared too. It had come as something of a jolt to learn that yet another member of his graduating class had left the ministry— this one now working in personnel management in the secular world. On the one hand, he felt that it was entirely possible for God to lead a man out of the ministry and into another job. But in too many of the cases he knew about, disillusionment and a lack of any active church affiliation following the break indicated that a fuller life of service to the Lord had not been the motivation.

The last few greeting cards were from relatives, and unlike most of the others in the stack, these had little religious content. Contrary to much popular opinion, ministers don't necessarily have any more Christian relatives than anyone else. Adam's mother and father, now dead, had been the only churchgoers in their families, and even they had not really become involved until Adam became a Christian as a college student. Soon after his decision for Christ his parents began attending a Bible study and gradually became more active.

When their son informed them that he felt God was leading him into full-time Christian work, they were less than enthusiastic. He had done well in school, and they had envisioned great things for him. As it became clearer that their boy would end up as a pastor, Clayton and Caroline Dunn, for the first time in their lives, actually paid attention at the annual meeting of the congregation and came to realize how much their church was paying their own pastor. They were surprised and outraged and said so; and perhaps startled at the outburst from such an unexpected quarter, the congregation voted to increase the pastor's proposed salary by one thousand dollars that year and repeated the increment for several years after that. After watching his parents' behavior, Adam wondered how salaries might be affected if all church members paid their ministers what they would want for themselves or their only sons.

The Christmas card from one of Trudi's aunts and uncles was a beautiful multicolored foil in the shape of a large partridge; the one from her sister and husband showed several reindeer standing one on top of the other in order to attach a star to the top of the tree. The final greeting card sported a tipsy Santa with a champagne glass in his hand and read, "It's Christmas, so have a ball!" That one was from cousin Mary, the daughter of his mother's younger sister. At the bottom of the card she had scrawled, "Mom's liver acting up again. Really worried about her, but nothing to do. Hope you're all well." Aunt Tina's liver had held up pretty well, considering, Adam mused. But it was ironic that Mary could think an inebriated Santa was funny after all she'd been through because of alcohol.

Trudi, walking through the family room on her way to the kitchen, stopped and asked, "What's the matter?"

"Nothing. Why?"

"Well, when I left you were looking like the cat that ate the canary. Now you look as if you've lost your best friend."

"Oh, it's just that you can't get away from it for very long. Even Christmas cards remind you of all the sadness around, even in the comparatively sheltered circle of our family and friends." Adam stretched out his arm, and when Trudi went over to sit on the arm of his chair, she found that, with Adam's help, she landed in his lap instead. "That's better!" he announced.

Trudi laughed. "We aim to please," she said, settling into the curve of his arm. And they sat there in front of the fire until dinner absolutely had to be started, trying to push the ghosts of other people's predicaments out of their conscious minds so that they could, for a while, at least, simply enjoy each other and savor the love-filled life the Lord was allowing them to live.

12

Be All Things to All Men

Leaning as far back in his desk chair as he could, Adam stretched. His body cried out for some exercise, and he really needed some, after all the rich Christmas food he had consumed. He had promised himself, during his years of schooling, that once he got out of seminary, the sedentary part of his life would diminish. Instead he sometimes felt chained to his desk, studying, writing letters, news releases, and other articles, telephoning, planning meetings—as he was now doing—and at night sitting still more during various kinds of gatherings.

It was taking him forever to put together the agenda for the January elders' meeting, and try as he might, he could find no way to pare it down any further. The monthly committee reports were indispensable, and the men would need some time for tying together the loose ends for the annual congregational meeting later in the month. In addition, there were several matters which they would have to settle sooner or later, and although Adam had decided to table them for the holidays, he was not sure they should be put off any longer.

He rubbed his burning eyes. The Kleinschmidt imbroglio, he had decided, did not need to be brought before the board. Christine still pleaded for absolute secrecy, and although Adam would not have thought it possible, the newspapers had protected the family's identity in its coverage and had not exploited the sensational aspects of Claus's hearing and trial. The news story was tucked away on the fourth page and would have escaped even Adam's notice if he had not been watching for it. Besides, Christine was considering moving to Hampton where her parents lived.

Sally had knocked briefly on the door and had entered with the mail. Seeing her boss tipped back in his chair and sensing that he was completely engrossed, she had laid the stack on his desk and gone back out without a word.

Adam now flopped down his chair to its normal position and gazed at the heap absently. Before long, however, the message of the postcard that lay on top impressed itself on his conscious mind, causing him to groan with annoyance. It read:

Adam:
    This is to remind you that during the month of January you have the privilege of representing the ministerial association by praying at the meetings of the board of education, the city council, and the coordinating council.

The times and places of the meetings were then listed, and Adam saw that, adding insult to injury, two of them fell on Monday, nicely ripping up his day off.

After stoically entering the dates in his appointment book, he returned to the mail and found that beneath the offending postcard lay an unopened envelope addressed to Mr. Adam Dunn and bearing no return address. This probably meant that it contained some anonymous message. No wonder Sally had sneaked in and out so quickly. Anonymous notes were rarely complimentary.

Adam slit open the envelope and extracted a short arti-

cle which had been torn somewhat crudely out of a
magazine he did not recognize. It was entitled "How to
Save Souls" and the bottom bore the inscription "Harry
Emerson Fosdick, *The Living of These Days*." Many
phrases of the piece had been underlined in ball-point
pen, either hastily or angrily. Adam laid back again in his
chair and read:

> The preacher's business is not merely to discuss
> repentance, but to persuade people to repent; not
> merely to debate the meaning and possibility of
> Christian faith, but to produce Christian faith in the
> lives of his listeners . . . .
> A good sermon is an engineering operation by
> which a chasm is bridged so that spiritual goods on
> one side—the "unsearchable riches of Christ"—are
> actually transported into personal lives upon the
> other.
> A justifiable criticism of much modern, liberal
> preaching is that, though it consists of neat, analyti-
> cal discourses, pertinent to real problems, and often
> well conceived and happily phrased, it does nothing
> to anyone. Such sermons are not sermons, but es-
> says, treatises, lectures. It is lamentably easy to
> preach about moral courage without making anyone
> more courageous; to deliver a discourse on faith
> without creating any of that valuable article in a
> single life; to argue that man has power to decide
> and choose without causing anyone then and there
> to make a momentous decision.

Clearly, last Sunday's sermon had missed the mark,
though how the dissection of a few verses in James could
be labeled "modern liberal preaching" momentarily escaped him. This letter was the kind of thing that had

devastated him as a brand-new minister. He could handle it with some sort of equanimity now, but how anyone so zealous for the cause of sound doctrine could be warped enough to use such unbiblical tactics was more than he could grasp.

Adam got up and went to his files, located the manila folder labeled "Pen Pals" and placed the clipping in front. Another letter caught his eye, and yet another, so he pulled out the entire collection and returned to his desk to peruse some long-forgotten communiqués.

Dear Rev. Dunn,

A written note of protest over the length of Sunday's church service. A protest I'm sure will have great impact on you from such a large giver.

As all red-blooded American males are aware, the hours after 12 on Sunday are reserved for napping in front of the turbulent tube, ostensibly watching a water-polo match from the isle of Japan, a sport about which he knows nothing. This past Sunday not only did I miss the TV nap, but I'm sure the effects of the service will disturb me all week, perhaps having some adverse effect on my health, and most certainly stirring my almost dead conscience.

My sincere and bountiful gratitude to an honorable minister as well as to a grand guy who has the veracity to act as well as speak.

Very truly yours,
Cam Allendorf

Dear Adam,

How can we ever thank you for your love and comforting presence in our hour of deep anguish? I only wish I had thought to have your beautiful meditation taped so I could hear it over and over. During the service I spent most of my time trying to hold up for the sake of others. Everyone was so shocked, I couldn't let myself go to pieces.

God's goodness has never failed. We all have had our moments of shattering grief, but never all at once, so we can always comfort one another. The great joy of knowing that Francie is safe and happy with God her Father and Christ her elder brother and all our loved ones who have gone on before sustains and blesses us. I feel for those who lose children if they are not sure of their salvation.

You mean so much to us. God bless you and keep you.

All our love,
Jim and Frances

Dear Rev. Dunn,
   i am Sorry i Took These ouT oF The ChuRch!
Will you please FoRgive me!

Love,
Dee Dee Miller

Dear Rev. Dunn,

Just in case I may be right in believing that a preacher needs appreciation now and then expressed with thoughtful intent—perhaps dug out just a little deeper from the bedrock of self than those perfunctory church-door "enjoyed your sermons" (although they are so necessary to both sayer and hearer), I want to tell you—because it helps *me* to tell you—that your message this morning has brought more light, more strength, and more meaning to my very conscious prayer effort than anything

I have read and been able to understand. I know that
God spoke to *me* through you, and I thank Him for it.

Very sincerely,
Jean Thomas

Dear Preach,

How is everything down your way? Okay up
here . . . . We all got home safely Saturday.

I do want to thank you for those six days that we
had in the mountains. My feelings for "Christianity"
. . . are so much greater . . . I hope I did not cause
you too much trouble.

If any time you are in Dillman, drop in and meet
my family.

Your Good Friend,
Joe (The Mop) Silverson

P.S. Please write to me . . . .

Dear Reverend Dunn,

Thank you for visiting our kindergarten class.

Jimmy E.

I thought you only worked on Sundays, but I guess
you work other times, too.

Cindy F.

I think your robe is pretty. I wish you wore it all the
time.

Penny M.

I thought you were God, but now I know you're not.

Jennifer A.

My kitty died. I hope it went to heaven.

Sarah M.

We learned the verse you told us, "Serve one another in love."

Bobby H.

Come back and see us sometime when you aren't busy.

Craig T.

Dear Rev. Dunn,

Jan and I want to thank you for the time and effort that you have put into helping us get a good start in married life.

We will try to remember all the things you have told us. See you in church.

Dean and Jan Baker

Adam forced himself to stop reading and gathered up the variegated and odd-sized pieces of paper and stuffed them back into the manila folder. He had to finish the docket for the elders' meeting before he left to go calling since Sally would need all afternoon in order to run it off and get it in the mail. If it was not sent out today, the elders would not receive it in time to study it before the meeting, in which case every topic would take even longer.

One piece of business demanded immediate attention. That was the request from the Chamber of Commerce for the use of Calvary Church's parking lot as the staging area for the Saint Patrick's Day Parade on Friday and Saturday, March 15 and 16. Adam writhed inwardly at all the commotion that would entail: broken sprinkler heads, trampling of shrubbery, crepe paper and discarded food containers everywhere, kids running in and out of the building to use the restrooms, horse droppings.

Another thing that rankled him was that he hardly felt they had a choice, since a subtle form of blackmail existed whenever requests came from worthwhile civic groups. People more or less looked upon church property as being available to the community, so that they would not so much be grateful if you said yes as they would be indignant if you said no. Besides, several church officers, not to mention members, belonged to the Chamber of Commerce, and so were caught in the dilemma familiar to pastors—deciding between what they really felt like doing and what people were trying to get them to do.

Why anyone apart from the Roman Catholics could get excited about Saint Patrick was more than this Protestant pastor could understand, anyway. Although the Catholics had a much larger parking lot than Calvary Church, they had been smart enough to build their church high up on a hill, not at all a convenient site for assembling floats.

Well, it was the elders' decision, and Adam was determined to keep his mouth shut and stay out of the debate if at all possible. He continually bore the responsibility for more tough decisions than he wanted to already, and he did not intend to go looking for yet more sticky situations in which to involve himself, especially when the spiritual significance was so nebulous.

In some ways it would be easier on him if the elders said yes. In that case his reception by the Chamber of Commerce board undoubtedly would be far more cordial when he arrived, later in the month, to offer prayer. They and the city-council members usually endured such ministrations with good grace, especially if they didn't take too long. The church was considered useful for providing the token religious touches most people found comforting as long as the borrowed preachers didn't get carried away and as long as they also let the community use their facilities when the need arose.

He added the last remaining items to the agenda, then got up and carried the completed papers to Sally in the outside office.

"I have something special for you," he announced, and set the handwritten notes ceremoniously on her desk.

"Just what I've always wanted," Sally replied unenthusiastically.

"It's sure been quiet around here. Have you been intercepting all the calls?"

"Yes, I knew you were trying to get that finished. No one was in a particular hurry, so I told them I'd give you their messages later."

"I appreciate that." He looked over the list Sally handed him.

"Well, I guess I'll go home . . . unless you think I need to call these other people right now. Would late this afternoon be soon enough?"

"I think so."

"Okay. Maybe I'll be back before you leave, then. Have a *lovely* afternoon," he teased motioning to the pile of work he had just given her.

"You're very kind," she responded with great dignity, then cheerfully waved him out the door.

13

Don't Turn Away Anyone

Wednesday morning was well under way, and Adam still had not begun his sermon outline. He jotted down the information the undershepherd had reported during his last telephone conversation:

> Connie Thurlow—Community Hosp. Danger of Miscarriage
> Roy Fenniman—St. Agnes Hosp. Mass in lower abdomen

He would see them in the afternoon.

Turning back to his Bible, he reread the passage of Scripture he would be preaching on Sunday. A button on the telephone began flashing again, then Sally buzzed. It was Beverly Dawson on line one, she informed him.

Adam punched the glowing square. "Hi, Beverly, how are you today?"

"I'm fine, Pastor Dunn. How are you?"

"Just fine."

"Good. Well, what I called about is that my next-door neighbor had a heart attack the day before yesterday. They took him to the hospital, and he seemed to be getting better. Then they said he had another attack while he was there, and even with all their equipment, they couldn't save him. He died yesterday afternoon." She

127

paused, waiting for a reaction.

"I'm sorry to hear that, Beverly. Anyone I know?"

"It was Marshall McDaniel."

"Doesn't ring a bell."

"You probably haven't met him. He wasn't very active in the community."

"I guess not, then."

"Anyway, his wife is naturally very upset, and they don't have any close family, so I'm trying to help with funeral arrangements. She said they hadn't gotten to know any minister since they moved here, and I told her I was sure you'd be glad to have the service, and I'd call you right away."

Adam had known for some time what was coming and tried to remain calm despite his dread of the ensuing dialogue. Perhaps this time he could make the person understand.

"You said 'since they moved here.' How long have they lived here?"

"Well, let's see . . . ." Beverly thought for a moment. "We moved here in August four years ago, and they were here then, so I'd say five or six years."

"They've lived here five or six years and haven't gone to church?"

"I guess not."

Adam sighed. "These situations are all very difficult for me, Beverly. You see, it really puts me in an uncomfortable position." He paused, and the silence told him she didn't see at all. "What I mean is, it's hard to conduct a service for a total stranger because a Christian minister, just by his presence, is indicating that the deceased person was a Christian."

"Oh, I don't think so. I mean, you don't have to say anything that isn't true. And really, he was a very nice person."

"I'm sure he was. Lots of nice people aren't Christians. But the trouble is, you can't have a funeral without *saying* something. And what do you say without implying that the man has gone to be with the Lord?"

"I don't know . . . just read the Bible and pray?"

"The difficult thing there is choosing which parts of the Bible to read. I'm certainly not going to hit a widow with passages telling what happens to those who die outside of Christ. But I can't get up and read all the Scriptures of hope of life with Christ after death at the funeral of a person who hasn't shown any interest in the Lord that anyone can remember. Do you see what I'm trying to say?"

"But *someone's* got to bury these people, don't they?"

"I suppose so, but the church is not a public agency. My job is to try to represent Jesus Christ and one particular group of His people. I can't bury all the unchurched people in town. I'd have no time for anything else."

Sally knocked on his office door and stepped inside. Adam put his hand over the telephone mouthpiece.

"Kristi Jorgensen and her fiancé are here," she whispered. Adam nodded and held up two fingers, signaling that he'd be done in a couple of minutes. Sally nodded and went back out the door.

When he brought his attention back to the telephone conversation, Beverly was saying, ". . . the church is supposed to reach out to those in need. What can I tell her? What can I give for a reason?"

"Just say I'm not able to do it. That's the truth, I'm not." He knew she was shocked at his heartlessness. "Listen, Bev, I know what you're feeling, because in the past I felt just like you do. I held several funerals for people I never met. I looked at it as a chance to show the love of God, prove God cares, and all that. But I never felt right about it. It seemed phony somehow. Then one

time a widow called me up the night before the funeral
to make sure I wouldn't let on during the service that I
didn't know her husband from Adam. That's when I
realized why I do not feel good about these kinds of
situations. You see, what people are really asking is that
the minister conspire with them to give a false impression. He's supposed to pretend he knows them, that everything is all right, that the person is going to heaven.
Now I ask you, is that honest?"

". . . I guess not . . . ."

"Another question: Why in the world would a family
that has no more interest in the Lord than your neighbors
have shown even *want* a Christian service?"

"Well . . . I guess they don't know who else to turn
to."

"There aren't many places to turn, that's true. I've
often wished there were some government officials des-
ignated to bury people, just like judges marry people,
but as far as I know, there aren't."

Beverly sighed."It seems pretty harsh, but I can see
what you're saying, only . . . ."

"Only you hurt for them. I know, Bev. It's tough. I feel
bad all the time about what people have to face without
Christ in their lives. Try to remember that Jesus had all
the compassion of God, but He refused His hope and
comfort to those who would not follow Him. He said to
let the dead bury their own dead. It's pretty hard to picture the apostle Paul lending his services to marry or
bury unbelievers. Someday Christ is going to ask me,
'Why did you do this in My name; why did you do that in
My name?' I don't want to have to answer, 'because I
was afraid people would be mad at me if I didn't' or,
'because I needed a little more money that month.' "

Bev sighed again. "It never even occurred to me that
there would be a problem."

"Don't worry. You're not alone. I get requests for this kind of thing all the time. Why don't you let the mortuary handle that part of the arrangements, too? They're used to it."

"They *are?*" She nearly shouted with relief. "Oh, I didn't know that! Well! That's great! Okay, I'll give them a call."

"Fine. And thank you for understanding."

"Sure. Thank *you*. Good-bye."

After he replaced the receiver, Adam took a deep breath. Then he went to his door, opened it, and greeted the young couple waiting outside.

"Hi, Kristi, how are you? Come on in."

Kristi greeted him, smiling, and the two visitors moved into the office.

"Pastor Dunn, this is Kevin Walker."

"Glad to meet you, Kevin."

"Glad to meet you, too, sir."

"Let's sit over here where we can be comfortable." Adam motioned toward the couch and took a chair for himself. He was favorably impressed with the two young people—Kristi, modest as ever and slightly flushed, as became a young woman in love; Kevin, obviously well-mannered and neatly dressed. It was a joy to see such a healthy, handsome couple. The scraggly specimens hanging on each other at the bus stops these days made the two facing him seem almost overly wholesome by comparison.

"I'm glad you could see us today," Kristi began. "I could come in almost anytime, but Kevin got home only because his midterms were over early."

Adam nodded. He knew that Kristi attended the nearby community college, while the young man lived at the state college several hours' drive away.

"What year are you?" Adam asked him.

"A senior. I'll graduate with a business degree in June."

"That will be a relief, I imagine."

"It sure will! I had thought I would go on for another year and get my masters. But if I can find a good job, I won't. I've had enough school to last me awhile!"

Adam laughed. "I know the feeling. The day I finished my final seminary exam was one of the greatest days in my life. I can still remember how I felt. Sort of like getting out of jail, I think. But we're not here to talk about school, are we?"

"No, sir." Kevin made the effort to take the lead. "Mrs. Jorgensen probably told you when she called that Kristi and I want to get married. It won't be until the fall, after I get out of school and get settled in a job, but Mr. and Mrs. Jorgensen wanted us to come talk to you right away."

"That is very considerate of all of you, and you might be surprised to learn, very unusual. People often call up and want me to marry them 'this Friday.' I confess I've never really gotten used to it. I don't marry them, of course, but I'm always surprised when someone comes at me that fast. Do you live here in town, Kevin?"

"Yes, when I'm not at school. Kristi and I went to high school together."

Adam realized Kevin was an intelligent young man, because he had foreseen and answered the next question: How long have you known each other?

"Do you attend church somewhere, Kevin?"

"No, sir, I don't. That's probably why the Jorgensens wanted us to see you this early. I know they're concerned because I don't go to church. I've tried to assure them that it really isn't important, but I can tell they don't see it that way."

Adam glanced over at Kristi. She was looking at her

fingers intertwined in her lap, and he felt tension in the way she sat.

"If Kristi wants to go to church, great," Kevin went on. "It's really no big deal. In fact, I want to have a church wedding," he concluded somewhat forcefully.

This statement captured Adam's interest. Such sentiments were rare among today's males, especially non-believers. "And why is that?" he asked.

"Well, I had a sociology course last year, and in one of the sessions they gave us statistics about marriages in our state that showed that eighty-five percent of the people who get married in churches stayed married, compared to fifty percent among those who don't."

Adam tried not to show his surprise at the shallow interpretation of figures Kevin's statement betrayed. A look at Kristi showed that she was no more analytical than her fiancé, for she was beaming at him with approval.

"Those statistics are encouraging," Adam ventured. "But, of course, the success of those marriages wasn't based on the kind of building in which the ceremony took place. They lasted because of the power of common goals and beliefs and the approval of parents and friends which accompanies the usual church wedding. If you take a couple standing in front of a judge at city hall and transplant them inside a church for the ceremony, the chances for a lasting relationship would not improve because the church building would not, in their case, represent common beliefs and so on."

Kevin frowned, trying to gauge the worth of this conclusion.

"But we do have common beliefs and ideals," Kristi put in. "We've discussed almost everything, and we feel the same way about nearly everything!"

". . . Except your Lord?" Adam watched as Kristi

flushed, and Kevin looked more pale and somewhat defiant.

"Kristi, it is my understanding that you committed your life to Christ several years ago. Is that correct?"

She nodded. "But I've explained all that to Kevin, and he understands it's important to me." She looked at her fiancé and smiled.

"What effect do you think it would have on your life together, Kristi, if you and Kevin spent it all living in different cities?"

Both young people looked completely puzzled. After a moment Kristi said, "I don't understand what you mean."

"Well, Kristi, I'm trying to make a point. You are a member of the Kingdom of God. And if you marry someone who is not a Christian, you will not just be living in different cities, you'll be living in different kingdoms! It would put a real strain on a marriage to have different kings." He could tell the young woman was beginning to view the problem more seriously than she had.

He went on. "I want you to know that I think you are special, attractive people. I like you both. But a strange thing happens to a lot of neat people after a few years of marriage." He turned to Kristi. "How long do you think you would really continue to get up and go off alone to church on Sunday mornings?" He looked at Kevin. "And how long would it be before you began to resent the way Kristi's church activities interfered with your weekend plans?"

Neither of the young people spoke.

"It gets even worse after children are born. I'm not making up all this. I'm telling you what I hear from broken-hearted men and women who have sat exactly where you're sitting and poured out their souls to me. After children come, the father naturally wants the children to be close to him, to be like him. And if the mother takes them off to church, he sees a part of their lives of which he's shut out. He doesn't like not sharing it and doesn't enjoy the mother's having an 'in' with the children that he doesn't have. When the children take part in church programs, he may attend, but these aren't his friends, and he feels out of place. And so a quiet, deadly struggle begins."

Kristi looked miserable. Kevin's ears were red, and Adam felt sorry for him. *Lord, help me say the right thing. Help me reach him for You,* he prayed.

"Kevin, has anyone ever told you what it really means to be a Christian? Do you understand that God has a plan for your life, and He wants to be a part of your life?"

"I think I understand what Christians believe. Kristi and I have discussed it." Adam didn't blame him for sounding rather stiff and defensive.

"Good. Then have you come to a place where you are willing to find out what God's plan for you might be?"

"I think my life is going okay as it is. I don't see what God could add to it, really."

"Do you ever feel guilty about some of your thoughts or actions, or sense you are carrying a burden you'd like to be rid of, or wonder how you would face God if you had to meet Him today?"

"Not really. I hear guys on TV or radio going on about the 'burden of sin' and all that, but compared to a lot of guys I know . . . I mean, I've never done anything really bad."

"Well, Kevin, God seems to think it's pretty bad when we don't think we need Him and go on living as if He doesn't exist."

Kevin frowned again in thought. After a while he said, "I don't really see what all the fuss is about. If religion means a lot to someone, fine. If not, fine. There have been a lot of religions that have been important to a lot of people, but none of them means more than another to me. I don't want anyone trying to pin me down. I want to keep my options open."

Adam shook his head ruefully. "That's where you and I are different. I don't have any options."

The young man looked at Adam curiously. "What do you mean?"

"Well, I've been trying to explain the importance of Christians marrying Christians, because the Bible forbids a Christian to marry anyone else."

Kevin's face displayed little emotion, but Kristi's eyes widened in surprise. "It does?" she asked.

"Yes, it does. God has always warned His people against intermarriage with unbelievers. That is why I have been trying to spark Kevin's interest in the Lord. He says he wants to keep his options open, but as a minister bound by the Word of God, I have no options in a situation like this."

They sat in silence for a few moments. Then Kristi said in a shaky voice, "Then you won't marry us?"

"I don't like to make it so final, Kristi. I would prefer to think that if you determine to do God's will and wait for His timing, His Spirit might work in Kevin's heart and cause him to want Christ in his life."

Kevin shook his head. "It just isn't that important," he insisted.

"It is to God," Adam said as gently as possible, "and it will be to Kristi . . . and sooner or later, to you, too." He turned to the lovely young woman sitting in confusion on the couch. "Kristi, it grieves me to say this, it really does, but it is my duty to tell you that you will be making a grave mistake if you enter into a marriage that God cannot bless. You may not believe me or your parents, if they have talked to you about this, but the pain will

come, and those who love you want to spare you . . . and
Kevin . . . the heartaches ahead if you ignore God's
warning."

Kevin stood. Kristi hastily gathered her purse and
jacket and got up also, so Adam joined them. "Could I
pray with you?" he asked.

"I think we'd better be going," Kevin said gruffly.

Adam held out his hand, which the young man shook
somewhat unwillingly. "Please don't hesitate to call if
you want to talk over anything," he said. And with a
half-hearted thank you they left.

After he had closed the door, Adam went to his desk
chair, flopped into it, and tipped it back into his favorite
position. He was frustrated, apprehensive, and, yes, angry. Frustrated because yet another set of parents—the
Jorgensens—had shirked their God-appointed duty to
put an early end to their child's relationship with a
non-Christian: Who could really expect a young person
to back out after things had progressed so far as to become engaged? He was angry because once more someone had dumped on him the responsibility for taking the
hard stand (Why don't you go talk to Pastor Dunn?) instead of having the courage to tackle the situation themselves. Did they think he was some kind of emotional
superman, so that the pressure of continually playing
policeman (Don't do that, or you'll get into trouble!) did
not weigh on him? If others could not tell a person no to
his face, why did they insist on believing it didn't bother
a minister to do it? Did they think he owned a magic
wand that could correct years of wrong decisions with
one painless wave?

Adam tried to shake off the sense of foreboding grow-
ing within him but failed. The Jorgensens had been
members of Calvary Church for many years and had de-
veloped close friendships within the fellowship. It

would take a great deal of Christian grace for them to remain on good terms with Adam if Kristi came home very upset. It would be extremely difficult to accept the fact that their pastor wouldn't marry their daughter, even if they themselves wished Kristi would break the engagement. It was like telling a person they were overweight or that their child was impossible. A person himself could comment on his "fat" or his "brat," but woe to anyone else who dared to do so! Would Vic and Sue Jorgensen be spiritually mature enough to cope with this, or would they quit the church in a bloodletting huff and provide Kristi and Kevin with the wedding of the century somewhere else?

Lord, be with the Jorgensen family in the coming days. Help Kristi to trust You and believe You will work everything for her good if she obeys You. I pray the same thing for myself, Lord. Keep me convinced that everything will work for my good if I am true to Your Word. Let no human pressure, no fear of the consequences, sway me from being faithful to Your commands. Protect Your church, Lord, from the disruption this kind of situation can cause if those involved decide to make an issue of it. And, Lord, open Kevin's eyes to see who You really are and cause him to feel a need for You in his life. Save him from his own self-satisfaction and use this crisis to make us all more useful to You. I pray in Jesus' name, Amen.

14

Get Your Head
Out of the Clouds

Two days after his session with Kevin and Kristi, Adam received word that his aunt was in critical condition; her damaged liver had ceased to function, and she was not expected to live much longer. Since Aunt Tina was his mother's sister, he had seen her quite often until his parents had been killed in a freeway accident a few years earlier. Adam had known about Tina's drinking problem since he had been old enough to be aware of such undercurrents in adult conversation, but it was never openly discussed in his presence. In later years, however, after his aunt had married Jason Sorrell, her addiction had been increasingly difficult to ignore as the couple exercised less and less discretion.

The relationship between the Dunns and the Sorrells had deteriorated for other reasons as well. Jason's temperament was changeable, and while he appeared happy-go-lucky some of the time, he could also be hostile and argumentative. It was impossible to tell which of the moods was his natural one and which was the result of alcohol. He worked in the construction industry and harbored a basic distrust of and resentment for anyone who did not earn his living with his hands. Since a college degree, in Jason's estimation, was not worth the paper it was written on, Adam, with his seven years of higher education, was the embodiment of all his uncle disdained. Although in his early fifties, Jason Sorrell had the tanned and hardened physique of a thirty-year-old. Only the generous amount of gray in the stubble of his often-unshaven face hinted at his real age.

Adam felt an inward conviction that he should go see his aunt. He was not sure what the two-hundred-mile round trip would accomplish, but he knew he had to undertake it anyway. He held fond memories of Aunt Tina from his childhood—she used to slip him quarters from time to time—but he had never been assured of her salvation. The very fact that Jason had called to inform the nephew of her condition indicated that some openness might remain.

Matthew was home sick with the flu, so Adam made the pilgrimage alone. Trudi's company would have eased the boredom of the miles on the highway, but perhaps it was just as well she couldn't come. Jason was even more sarcastic toward Adam when Trudi or the boys were around to hear his barbed comments.

When Adam pulled up in front of his aunt and uncle's house, he was surprised to find Jason's car in the driveway. He had expected one of Tina's grown daughters to be there, perhaps, or to learn from a neighbor which hospital his aunt had entered. Instead, he soon discovered that the woman was lying at home in bed deathly ill with only her half-inebriated husband to tend her. Beer can in hand, Jason, dressed in white T-shirt and jeans, opened the screen door at Adam's knock, then turned and walked back into the front room without so much as a word of greeting.

"How's Aunt Tina?" Adam asked.

"Dying, just like I said on the phone." He jerked his head in the direction of the front bedroom.

Adam went over to the door, and despite the stench that assailed him through its partial opening, went in. His aunt was bloated nearly beyond recognition, and from the basin resting by her head, it was obvious that she had been vomiting. Adam drew closer and leaned over the slack form. "Aunt Tina?" he said softly. There was no answering movement. "Aunt Tina?" he said more loudly. The woman stirred fretfully and muttered something unintelligible in a whiny tone. Adam stood for a moment looking at this stranger, trying to remember what she really looked like, then returned to the front room where Jason slouched on the couch, nursing his beer. "Pretty bad, huh?" he commented.

"Why isn't she in a hospital?"

"What for? She's dying anyway. The doctor can't do nothin' for her."

"The doctor's been here?"

"Sure he's been here!"

"When?"

"Couple of days ago. Told us her liver and kidneys were probably all shot. Just a matter of time. I coulda' told you that without wastin' all that money on a house call, but Mary insisted."

"Where is Mary?"

"At the store. She's stayed here all night the last two days so she could be here when her mother called. She's the only one Tina wants around her," he added petulantly.

"Tina ought to be in the hospital."

"Why? So I can give all my hard-earned money to a bunch of dopes who can't do nothin' anyway? Nothin' doin'."

"She can't get proper care here, Jason. She's in bad shape. Didn't the doctor tell you she should be in the hospital?"

"Of course he did! What else would you expect? They're all in cahoots with each other, tryin' to clean out your pockets any way they can. Mary can do anything that needs to be done. Tina ain't conscious much, anyway." The man hoisted himself to his feet and went to the kitchen for another beer.

Adam followed him into the room which was littered with the remains of several meals, becoming more angry by the minute. "She needs to be in a hospital! They can give her medications to make her more comfortable. They can keep her clean, for one thing!"

Another can of beer hissed open, and Jason took a long swig, then eyed the younger man challengingly. "What's wrong? Can't you take it? What do you think they did before there *were* any hospitals? They made do at home, just like we're doing."

His nephew fought down his still-rising emotions. "They had to. We don't."

Through the front-room window Adam saw a car draw to the curb in front of the house. He recognized his cousin Mary, Tina's twenty-four-year-old daughter, as she got out of the car and lifted a bag of groceries out of the backseat. Grateful for the interruption, he went outside.

"Hello, Mary," he called. "Can I help you carry something?"

Mary set the bag on a fender and pushed her dark hair back out of her eyes. "Hi, Adam. There's another sack in there if you don't mind."

"Not at all. But let's talk for a minute first." He looked at her closely. "How are you doing?"

She smiled wanly. "Oh, I'm okay. How's Mom?"

"Probably about the same."

"I thought when I first saw you that maybe she had . . . gone."

"No, no. I just came to see if there was anything I could do. Jason seems to be in rare form."

Mary shook her head in disgust. "He's worse than no help at all. He hasn't been without a drink in his hand for two days."

"Mary, your mother should be in a hospital."

Tears filled the young woman's eyes. "I know it."

"Why don't you call an ambulance and have her admitted?"

Mary shook her head again. "Jason says she'll die if we try to move her, and he's probably right."

"Mary, if she stays *here*, she'll die."

"Well, he's her husband, and he says no."

"If you want her in, I'll get her in."

"Jason said he wouldn't pay for it. He went and took all their money out of the bank yesterday, so it wouldn't be tied up when she . . . ." Mary looked away quickly, biting her lower lip.

Furious at the capricious pigheadedness and lack of human feeling of the man swilling away in the house, Adam reminded himself that his aunt had, of her own free will, chosen to marry him, probably because he was such a willing drinking partner. Family members cannot protect each other from the results of such foolishness, he told himself, no matter how much they might wish to do so.

"If we put your mother into a hospital, he'll pay," Adam stated grimly. "His union must have hospitalization, anyway."

"He says it's only in effect when he's employed. He doesn't work steadily in the winter months, and he's off now." She wiped her eyes and blew her nose.

"Mary, quit worrying about Jason. If you want your mother moved, we'll get her there if I have to call the police!"

"It's just that it's impossible to do anything for her here! She can't keep anything down. She can't use a bedpan. I don't know what I'm doing! I've never taken care of a sick person before!" The girl's voice cracked in exasperation.

"I can't be the one to say, Mary. It will have to come from you."

"Jason won't let us move her."

"He won't do anything but yell. Don't let him fool you. He's not nearly as tough as he wants you to think he is. If he were, he wouldn't need his liquid crutch."

Mary began crying again and after some inward struggle whispered in a hesitant voice, "Get Mom to the hospital."

"She *may* die if we try to move her. Can you handle that? I mean, you've got to face the possibility and not blame yourself if that happens. The only way Jason can hurt you is to put something like that on you."

"Yes, I see that. No, if she should . . . die . . . moving her, I'd feel better having tried to help her than going on like this."

"Okay, let's take this stuff in. I'll keep Jason occupied while you call an ambulance. Maybe you'd better call from a neighbor's. Do you know anyone well enough?"

"I think so."

"Okay, then. We'll put the groceries in the kitchen, and then you just go quietly out the back door and to the neighbor's."

When the ambulance stopped in front of the Sorrells' house, children appeared as if from thin air, gathering around the doors, peering inside, watching, with wide-eyed fascination, every movement of the uniformed men. When Jason grasped what was happening, he went into a sputtering rage, but the attendants, recognizing his alcoholic condition, ignored him and completed their task efficiently. Though their comments to each other revealed their revulsion at the neglected appearance of the patient, they had Tina bundled into the back of the vehicle before her husband could find a way to impress them that he was the one who had the say and not the determined young man to whom they had looked for instructions.

When the ambulance had left, lights and siren operating furiously, Adam turned to his stepuncle. "I'm driving Mary to the hospital. Do you want to come with us?" He expected the older man to yell at him, or stalk back into the house, or perhaps even try to hit him. Instead, Jason stood swaying slightly on the sidewalk, staring at him with an expression almost like fear in his eyes. Mary, Adam realized, was trembling, so he opened the car door and helped her inside. Now that the confrontation was over, he felt a little shaken himself. He turned and spoke almost as he would have to a child. "Get into the car, Jason."

Still clinging to a beer can, his uncle, suddenly looking older than his fifty years, climbed into the backseat. Adam leaned in. "Do you have your wallet with you? You might as well try your insurance number." Jason shook his head. "I'll get it for you. Where is it?"

Jason stared unseeing at the container hanging in his hands between his knees. "On the dresser."

Adam returned to the house, located the wallet in the disheveled room, locked the doors, and went out to the car.

They reached the hospital much later than the ambulance and drove to the emergency entrance. The staff of the emergency section was fully occupied, and it was about fifteen minutes before Adam could even ascertain that his aunt had arrived and was in the examining room. The nurse handed him a clipboard with an admittance form on it which he took into the waiting room. Jason remained withdrawn; so Adam gave the information sheet to Mary to fill out. After the formalities were concluded, Adam called Trudi to report on the situation and asked her to let Sally know that he probably would not get to the office at all.

The three of them waited for nearly two hours. Jason at first sat as if in another world, but as the minutes dragged on, he became restless, then irritable, then belligerent. Adam made a few attempts to keep him from harassing the nurses, but after a while gave up. If the man grew too obnoxious, the hospital staff surely would know what to do with him better than Adam did.

Finally, when even Adam was about ready to demand some specific information, a man dressed in operating-room garb appeared. After determining who they were, the doctor looked sternly at the husband. "I'm sorry to tell you, sir, that your wife died a few minutes ago." Mary covered her mouth with her hand and began to weep quietly, but neither Jason nor Adam registered much emotion at the news.

"She was in extremely critical condition when she arrived. She should have been brought in long before now." The man sounded almost angry. Perhaps he was, Adam thought. "Her veins were so bad that we couldn't even get an IV in," he went on. "We called the physician listed on the admittance sheet, and he said he urged you to bring her in two days ago." He paused and waited for some reaction. Receiving none, he continued. "At any rate, we have enough information that I think an autopsy won't be necessary."

Feeling that one of them ought to vocalize something, Adam said, "Thank you anyway for your efforts."

The doctor nodded briefly at him, looked at the other two, then shrugged. "The husband will have to come back tomorrow to sign papers and tell us what to do with the body," he announced abruptly, and left.

All the way back to the Sorrells' house, Jason held forth on the stupidity of the medical profession, the uselessness of the trip to the hospital, and the comparative adequacy of the care Tina had received at home. During the monologue, Adam prompted Mary into deciding which girl friend she should stay with for a few days. When they reached the house, his cousin got out quickly, went to her own car, and drove off.

Jason opened the back car door, but remained sitting on the backseat while he vented his spleen at his nephew's interference. Finally he got out, started to shut the door, then thought better of it. Leaning back in, he looked at Adam and smiled unpleasantly.

"Well, at least this all accomplished one thing," he said, his voice dripping with contempt. "At least it got you down out of that preacher's ivory tower of yours, so you can see what the world is really like!" Then he slammed the door shut as hard as he could and walked stiffly into the house.

15

Never Give Up Hope

Sitting at his desk on Saturday morning, which had dawned bleak and cold, Adam's mind kept straying from the sermon he was trying to study, bent instead on rehashing his disturbing encounters of the week. Muffled sounds occasionally reached him from other parts of the building, no doubt caused by Sunday-school teachers and the custodian preparing for the following day's activities. The commotion outside created by the workers putting finishing touches on the Saint Patrick's Day floats could not last forever—the parade started at one o'clock.

He had heard nothing from the Jorgensens, and he did not know whether that was good or bad. He had been praying continuously, it seemed, for them and his cousin Mary, who would have difficulty emerging from the trauma of the last few days. He had tried also to pray for Jason but could not quite bring it off; he formed the words asking for his stepuncle's salvation, but the faith to believe it could actually happen simply was not there.

How successful Roy Fenniman's colostomy had been was not yet known. At best, weeks of radiation treatments lay ahead. Connie Thurlow had been sent home but had to stay in bed for at least three weeks, and perhaps three months if her condition did not improve. Matt had passed his virus on to Tim and, possibly, Trudi.

She had not been feeling well when he left for the office, and someone probably would have to step in and teach her class of seventh-grade girls tomorrow.

The last six months had produced the usual hodge-podge of human activity, with Pastor Dunn fluctuating from the role of the victim to that of the prophet in the various dramas. The months before that, the year even further back, all contained their quotas of quandaries and crises, most of which Adam could recall dimly if at all. Some disastrous situations, such as the drowning of a baby in a swimming pool, the attempted suicide of a teenager, the psychotic woman who believed one of the laymen was requesting that certain songs be played to her over the radio, these loomed closer to the surface of the conscious mind. But the steady stream of couples with marital problems, each certain theirs was a unique situation when in fact most recited a familiar story of selfishness and pride—these melded into a single body of pain. Whenever he paused to reflect on all the misery, it became one collective deadweight to his soul, a drag on his creative energies.

Most of these cries for help came from the great mass of society—people who generally considered the church to be far removed from the realities of their lives. But when their pain became too great, and they had tried everything else they could think of, they came trotting around to unload on the first preacher who came to mind. Perhaps one out of ten responded to the scriptural reme-dies suggested to them. But the great majority dropped from sight as soon as they had exhausted the resources the fellowship of the church offered them. If it became clear that an alleviation of their situation would demand some change or sacrifice on their part, they simply dis-appeared. Adam's card file was filled with the names of those he had counseled, called on, and prayed for, who had gone their own way and would never be heard from again. He wished he knew where the ivory tower Jason talked about was located. He'd like to climb up into it and stay there until the Lord returned.

The rather loud rap on his office door jolted Adam out of his mental rummaging. *What now?* he thought. *Lord, I really can't take another downer.* He got up and went to the door.

Opening it, he found, to his surprise, the tall gangling frame of Larry Jacobs, his secretary's son. He was a good-looking and muscular young man, with a shock of auburn hair as one of his more distinctive features.

"Larry! How're you doing?"

"Fine, Pastor Dunn. Do you have a few minutes to talk to me?"

"Sure! Come on in! I thought maybe your mom had sent you over with something for me."

"No, I just wanted to talk to you, and Saturdays are about the only time I'm free."

As they sat down, Adam wondered, as he often did, where the boy got his genes; neither Sally nor Dan had any of the look of the basketball player about them. "I'm glad to see your team is doing so well."

"Yeah, it's great. But rough. The finals are a lot tougher than the regular games. I got a finger in my eye last night and had to go out. For about five minutes I thought I was going to die."

"How's it feeling today? I see it's pretty bloodshot."

"The doc says it's okay. I've got some stuff to put in it. It stings some, but doesn't really bother me."

"I'll bet it's hard to maintain a Christian witness under the basket, especially with someone's finger in your eye."

Larry's lightly freckled face lit up in an infectious grin. "Yeah, it is, but only for the first few seconds. And the

Lord seemed to take care of them."

"Good."

"That's kind of what I wanted to talk to you about. I've been doing a lot of thinking lately about what I really want to do with my life. I've always thought, you know, that the greatest thing in the world would be to play professional basketball, but lately I've been wondering, you know, if that's really where it's at for me."

"You're a senior, aren't you?"

"Yes. I turn eighteen next month."

"Do you have any definite college plans?"

"Well, there's a couple of schools looking at me for scholarships, but if nothing comes of that, I'll probably go to the state college and, you know, try to make the team there."

"It would sure be great if you got a basketball scholarship!"

"Yeah, it would, but . . . I'm trying not to count on it."

"At any rate, you're not sure you want to continue in basketball as a career even if you could?"

"No. You see," Larry sat forward and spoke earnestly, "the most satisfying thing in my life right now is when I can tell somebody about Jesus Christ and see Him change his life. And I'm beginning to wonder if maybe God wants me to be a minister, so I can spend all my time leading people to Christ!"

The final words hit a raw nerve inside Adam, and it was several moments before he could respond. Larry had echoed Adam's own vision when he had first contemplated God's call for a church vocation. If only he *could* spend all his time leading people to Jesus instead of getting bogged down with forms, feelings, and situations so tangled that even coming to Christ could not completely unravel them! Yet it was true that a pastor undoubtedly had more opportunities to touch more people with the Gospel than other Christians. He had worked in the secular world long enough before seminary to realize how very hard it was to get a word of witness in edgewise.

He looked at the eager, manly face in front of him. *O Lord,* he thought, *if You are still speaking to such young people as this, there is hope for this world yet. Don't let me say anything that will quench his zeal or tarnish the dream You have given him.*

"It's wonderful to hear you say that, Larry," Adam heard himself answering and meant it. "I know the Lord has really used you here at church already and that your leadership has been a vital part of the impact of our high-school program. Some people seem to think that they will start evangelizing when they graduate from seminary, as if at that moment something switches on, and they become a powerful servant of God. That's not the way it is. If a person isn't actively witnessing before he becomes a pastor, he's not likely to start afterward."

"Then you think the Lord may be calling me into the ministry?"

"Yes, He *may* be. He might also be testing your willingness to do whatever He wants, so you can know for sure that you are not making a god out of basketball or anything else."

"I can see that. To tell you the truth, it was a struggle for a while."

"I'm sure it was. But He won, and He knows it, and you know it, and now I know it, and I appreciate your sharing it with me. I'll join you in praying for further enlightenment over the coming months and years."

"I haven't said anything yet to Mom and Dad. I thought I'd bounce it off you first."

"Well, I don't want you to feel locked into this, like I'm going to think you've reneged if God leads you in a different direction." Adam paused, then continued, carefully choosing his words. "And maybe I ought to say also that being a pastor does not mean you spend all your time telling people about Jesus. Unfortunately, the ones most anxious to hear about Him are generally those who know Him. Frankly, many of the people who come in here have their minds made up about something they want me to do for them and won't even listen to me if I try to bring the Lord into our conversation."

"That's how it is at school! The kids want to tell me all their troubles but tune me out if I mention God, church, or anything like that."

"Then you'll understand if I say that adults are just teenagers who are a few years older and probably not anymore willing to admit their need and turn to the Lord than your friends are."

"That's bad." Larry pondered this information seriously for some time. Then he asked, "So what does a preacher do about it?"

Adam laughed. "I've been trying to figure that out for years! I guess just plug away at the unsaved and problem Christians the best you can, and find your joy in those who do come to faith and in those who continue to grow, year in and year out, as they hear and follow God's Word." *Yes, Lord*, he thought, *that's what we have to do. But it sounds so easy in capsule form, and it's so perturbing one day at a time.*

Larry sat digesting Adam's words, and perhaps adjusting his dream a bit. His pastor went on, "But someone has to be the preacher, teacher, counselor. And if God is calling you to do that, you won't be happy doing anything else, and He *will* use you to reach others for Him." Adam grinned. "Maybe He will even reward you by sending in a neat young basketball player to encourage your heart and give you hope for the future."

Larry blushed until he almost matched the red letterman's jacket he was wearing. "I came in for myself, but if it's done something for you, then that's cool."

Adam leaned forward. "You've made my day. Let's pray together, shall we?"

After Larry left, Adam lay back in his tilted chair and enjoyed the glow the young man's visit had sparked. The same principle held true for pastors as for lay people: it was your relationships with other Christians, the sharing of the inner life of the Body of Christ, that poured oil on your wounded spirit and restored your soul. He was grateful as he thought of the many Christian friends from whom he and Trudi drew refreshment and strength when they became spiritually worn down.

Adam was still languishing in this rather blissful state when his telephone light began flashing, and he heard its bell jangling out in Sally's empty office. He leaned forward and lifted the receiver. "Calvary Church, Pastor Dunn speaking."

"Reverend Dunn? This is Tom Glover. I tried to call you at home, and your wife gave me this number."

"That's fine. What can I do for you?"

"Well, I'm the president of the Little League here in town, and I understand that one of your boys is signed up this year."

"That's right. I'm one of the assistant coaches, or whatever you call them."

"Great. Well, what I called about is, we're having the opening-day ceremony the middle of next month, and we were wondering, since you have a boy in the program, if you'd say the prayer at the ceremony for us . . . ."